Zen: Beginner's Guide

Happy, Peaceful ar yone

Positive Psychology Coaching Series

Copyright © 2015 by Ian Tuhovsky
Author's blog: www.mindfulnessforsuccess.com

All rights reserved. No part of this publication may be reproduced, stored in a retrieval system, or transmitted, in any form or by any means, electronic, mechanical, photocopying, recording or otherwise without the prior written permission of the author and the publishers.

Table of Contents

Introduction 5
Chapter 1: Why Zen? **8**
Chapter 2: What is Zen Buddhism? **13**
    What Zen Buddhism is NOT? 14

    Where Did Zen Come From? 15

    What Does Zen Teach? 16

    What is Meditation All About? 21

    How does One Meditate in Zen? 25

    Zen Principles 42

Chapter 3: Living Zen **69**
    How to Slow Down 74

    Mindfulness on Steroids 77

    Celebrate! 79

    A Few Simple Techniques (and some more life philosophy) .. 80

    Avoiding Drama 84

    Pleasure is NOT Happiness 87

    Accept Everything, Lose Nothing 89

    Six Ways to Practically Let Go 90

    Why is Being Alone a Good Thing? 100

    De-clutter and Live Simply 106

Chapter 4: Where Do I Start? **114**
Conclusion **120**
    Hey there like-minded friends, let's get connected! 122

Recommended Reading For You **123**
About The Author **135**

My Free Gift to You
Discover How to Get Rid of Stress & Anxiety and Reach Inner Peace in 20 Days or Less!

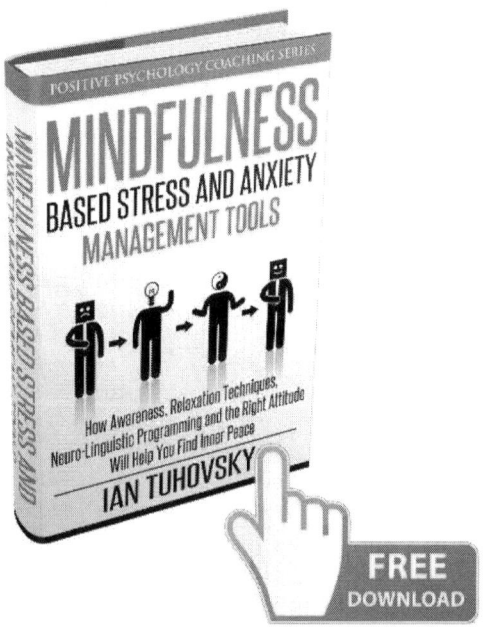

To help speed up your personal transformation, I have prepared a special gift for you!

Download my full, 120 page e-book "Mindfulness Based Stress and Anxiety Management Tools" (Value: $9.99) for free.

Moreover, by becoming my subscriber, you will be the first one to **get my new books for only $0.99,** during their short two day promotional launch. **I passionately write about**: social dynamics, career, Neuro-Linguistic Programming, goal achieving, positive psychology and philosophy, life hacking, meditation and becoming the most awesome version of yourself. Additionally, once a week I will send you insightful tips and **free e-book offers** to keep you on track on your journey to becoming the best you!

That's my way of saying **"thank you"** to my new and established readers and helping you grow. I hate spam and e-mails that come too frequently – **you will never receive more than one email a week! Guaranteed.**

Just follow this link:

http://www.mindfulnessforsuccess.com/positive-psychology-coaching/giveaway.html

Please be aware that every e-book and "short read" I publish is written truly by me, with thoroughly researched content 100% of the time. Unfortunately, there's a huge number of low quality, cheaply outsourced spam titles on Kindle non-fiction market these days, created by various Internet marketing companies. I don't tolerate these books. I want to provide you with high quality, so <u>if you think that one of my books/short reads can be improved anyhow, please contact me at:</u>

contact@mindfulnessforsuccess.com

<u>I will be very happy to hear from you, because that's who I write my books for!</u>

Introduction

Ever wonder why the heck you are multi-tasking your butt off, but don't feel accomplished? Do you feel like you have factors in your life that should make you happy, but you just aren't? Is making a simple decision excruciatingly difficult for you? Is your mind full of swirling thoughts, and your gut full of worry and regret?

If you answered yes to any of these questions, you are a normal member of western society. But who wants to be normal?

I too, was "normal." But guess what? Nowadays, normality is settling for less than we deserve. And I don't know about you, but I was working my butt off to *not* settle, yet I was never happy. I lived a busy, unhappy, "normal" life… and I was miserable. Normal does not mean natural.

To live Zen is to live the most natural life, the way that we were designed to live; experiencing every moment, in the moment. Taking up a Zen practice will not solve all of your problems but it enables you to solve your problems, without the past obscuring your decisions. And most of the time what we see as a "problem" in our western society is anything but. Zen will give you a completely new perspective on life; one that allows you to live life to the fullest!

In this book I will explain to you all about Zen and how it will connect you with your natural self. I explain how Zen enables us to find our true self, within, which is present here and now. No more waiting, no more confusion, no more wasting away your life!

You will learn all about Zen and its practical uses in everyday life for "normal," regular, everyday people, and how it will inevitably change the way that you look at and experience life… FOREVER. I will go over:

- A short history and explanation of Zen
- The major teachings and precepts of Zen
- Zen meditation techniques that are applicable and practical
- The benefits of a Zen lifestyle
- How to accept everything and lose nothing
- How to de-clutter your life
- Why being alone can be beneficial
- How to avoid drama
- Any many more…

Before we begin: This is not just another "traditional Zen" encyclopedia essay or a purely informative style book. If you want to read about the history of Zen in detail, I recommend that you grab some other book. If you want to learn about traditional Buddhism and its various branches in general -<u>I wrote another book just on this fascinating topic.</u>

The purpose of this work is to show you how to apply and utilize the teachings and essence of Zen in everyday life in the Western society. I'm not really an "absolute truth seeker" unworldly type of person - I just believe **in practical plans and blueprints that actually help in living a better life.** If Zen wasn't that, you wouldn't be reading this book now. Of course I will tell you about the origin of Zen and the traditional ways of practicing it, but I will also show you my side of things, my personal point of view and translation of many Zen truths through a more "contemporary" and practical language. **It is a "modern Zen lifestyle" type of book.**

Thanks again! I hope you enjoy reading!

Chapter 1: Why Zen?

At the age of 26, I believed I was "living the life." I had a full-time career as a headhunter, great friends and a wonderful girlfriend. I was very productive in my own mind, as I was constantly busy with commitments. I was on the go all the time. Multi-tasking was my middle name, and my "to-do list" always got completed. Yet, I would often stop to wonder, "If my life is so fulfilled, if I am truly 'living the life,' then why am I tired, stressed, confused, and downright miserable? What am I missing?"

The answer to this question was given to me by example, instead of by word of mouth. Zen. It wasn't much of a fancy story, just a usual event that has led me to something bigger. My childhood best friend had moved across the country. We interacted over six years through email, text, and video chat.

He always looked happy, spoke positively, and had a peace about him. I thought maybe he was on the newest anti-depressant, smoked a lot of drugs, or maybe he was secretly making tons of money. Either way, we planned a reunion weekend. He was coming to my town for a week.

Now, granted, I may have been able to get a lot done back then, but I was hardly a decisive person. I was always worried about the repercussions of my decisions. I would over think everything, wondering "Is this a bad choice or a good choice?" I would think about past experiences similar to a problem I was facing and burn myself out coming up with different scenarios according to how things might pan out. Oh, this was only for major decisions relating to life changing things, right? No. I went through this process every day, all day long. From what to order on the menu, to which grocery store to go to, I was constantly confused with my own thinking.

As my pal and I were catching up over dinner (where it ceremoniously took me a half hour to pick out my entrée), he asked why I looked so stressed out. I explained to him that I really didn't know. Then I laughed and said: "Whatever you're are on, I want some." He smiled and told me that he decided years ago to live and experience life. I was confused. I almost felt like I had to defend myself. I went through the motions of explaining all that I do every day; how much I multi-task; how much I *think*! "I am living *way* more life than you," I told him. Little did I know how wrong I was.

That night, after a few beers, he shared with me his little secret. Zen. It was not just for Buddhist monks on a hillside monastery somewhere, like I previously imagined. It is not some hocus pocus, religion requiring the raking of sand and the wearing of sheets. It is living and experiencing every moment of life just as it is. It requires no fight, little thought, and a lot of practice.

Fast forward seven years. I love my life. Granted, I may not "get done" as much as I used to (which meant focusing at one hundred areas of my life at once, which leads nowhere). Yet, I am able to make decisions with ease. I do not regret my past nor do I fret about my future. I just am. I live. And guess what? I am truly happy. I am now "living the life."

Zen is an absolutely practical and useful lifestyle for everyone. Through meditation, enlightenment is found. Yet, it is not a moment of enlightenment that we seek in Zen. Enlightenment is lived every day, we seek to live an enlightened *life*, not to experience a moment of awakening.

My life has changed in so many ways. I had no other choice BUT to write this book. I do not want anyone else to have to continue through life without actually being able to *live* it. A life not lived is much worse than death. I have to share all that I have learned because even if it changes one person's life, as it has mine, it will be enough.

Zen Facts

Here are some important facts about Zen Buddhism that you probably don't know:

- Zen Buddhism is not a religion. Anyone practicing another religion may practice Zen at the same time!

- Zen Buddhism is based around meditation, but not your average type of mediation. It largely revolves around periods of sitting meditation, but incorporates many techniques, allowing you to essentially meditate all day long!

- Zen could also be termed "the study of living." It's also about the right point of view and the right perception of the reality (right = among many others, the perception that serves your happiness and clarity of intent, unbiased by unnecessary judgments, social conditioning etc.).

- Zen will connect you with your natural, true self; free of past trauma, labels, and mistakes you have made.

Zen meditation methods are practical and beneficial for everyone. By using these techniques, and by putting them into practice in your everyday life, you will:

- Gain self-trust
- Gain wisdom
- Gain a true sense of happiness
- Have better relationships with others
- Have an easier time ridding yourself of addictions
- Be able to rid yourself of depression
- Become mentally stronger
- Reduce stress
- Learn to be an optimist
- Rid yourself of wandering, racing thoughts
- Be able to sleep better

- Have an easier time making decisions

Zen is freedom, happiness, truth, living, wisdom, peace, tranquility, stillness, letting go, and so much more. It's a perfect lifestyle. All of these things that we have been looking for in other places have been available all along, closer than we thought. They are all found in YOU (well, and me)! Living a practical Zen life will help you to see that *you* hold the key to your own happiness.

Chapter 2: What is Zen Buddhism?

Contrary to popular belief, Zen is not a discipline reserved for monks practicing Kung Fu. Although there is some truth to this idea, Zen is a practice that is applicable, useful, and practical for anyone to study regardless of what religion you follow (or don't follow).

Zen is the practice of studying your subconscious and seeing your true nature. Our true nature is devoid of past experiences and feelings or ideas that we have developed during our lives. Despite the ideas that people have about Zen being mystical and other-worldly, it is actually one of the most simple, down to earth practices around. For the most part, we are all quite ordinary on the inside. Many people believe that Zen is about having supernatural, spiritual experiences: visions, revelations, etc. In all actuality, living Zen is about experiencing regular, every day moments, with your feet on the ground, 24/7.

Zen is also the act and discipline of having undeviating experience with our lives as we are living them, day to day. It truly is the "practice of living." When we live Zen, we are fully in tune with what we are doing and have nothing unnecessary on our minds in the meantime. We are experiencing things around us just as they are.

What Zen Buddhism is NOT?

Zen is not a belief system, philosophy, or religion; it is a practice. Zen is a school of Buddhism, yet one can practice Zen without being a Buddhist. Likewise, one can be a Buddhist without practicing Zen. This holds true with all religions. We have the ability to belong to any religion we like while still practicing Zen.

Being that Zen is not belief based, therefore it is not necessary to have faith in outlandish, other worldly things that are difficult to wrap our minds around. The only thing you need to *want* to believe is that you have a true nature. You must have faith that this nature is within yourself, buried under all of the experiences you have had in your life that previously influenced who you were.

Zen is not about doing or attaining something. "The destination is the journey." Practicing Zen is not about reaching an end, be all goal. It is commonly thought that there is an objective to meet when studying and living Zen: enlightenment. Yet, enlightenment is not reaching some huge, mystical climax.

Zen is not about experiencing a *moment* of enlightenment, it is about living a lifetime of enlightenment! I will discuss enlightenment later so that you may understand it better and rid yourself of preconceived ideas tied to the word.

Zen is not about rational, active thinking. It is not about what you think. If you intellectualize anything it will hinder your practice of Zen. Instead, you need to learn how to calm and quiet your logical, thinking mind. You will be running off of intuition, which requires no deliberate effort.

Zen is not complicated, it is very simple. Zen is experiencing being alive and all that comes with it, right now. Practicing Zen may be hard for some at first, but many new things are. That is why practice is necessary. We have developed bad habits like holding on to past experiences and over-thinking everything. Bad habits take time and effort to get rid of, just like acquiring a new habits does. The process may be a little bit difficult, but not complex in the least and totally worth it.

Where Did Zen Come From?

Zen is a branch of Mahayana Buddhism. It was brought to China roughly 15 centuries ago, in 6 CE. Zen was brought to China by Indian Buddhist monk, Bodhidharma. There it was known as "Ch'an," which is the Chinese interpretation of Sankrit term, "dhyana," meaning a mind that is immersed in meditation. The term we know now, Zen, is the Japanese pronunciation of "Ch'an."

Bodhidharma went to the Shaolin Monastery in China, bringing the teachings of Zen with him. Fun fact: this is how Zen came to influence Kung Fu. Bodhidharma is still known as the "First Patriarch of Zen."

In Japan, teachings of Taoism and Buddhism were already starting to blend. Bodhidharma's lessons were along some of the same lines, so they converged easily, and were easily accepted thanks to the Tao/Buddhist influence.

Slowly but surely, many of the Indian ideas in Zen were cast off. They were slowly phased out by Chinese influences and what we commonly recognize as Zen principles. This is largely credited to Zen's sixth patriarch, Huineng. He taught at the beginning of what is known as Zen's Golden Age. The influences of this age are still taught and felt in modern day Zen, passed down in tales and the koans used for meditation.

Zen was divided into five different schools during this period. The Rinzai and Soto schools are still widely practiced today and are very distinct. I will discuss both in more detail later in this book as they are very important.

Zen spread to Vietnam early on, probably around the 7th century. Korea received Zen during the Golden Age. Because of the World War II and globalization, westerners were able to get a taste of eastern culture, including Zen. Since then, Zen has become an established practice in the West as well.

What Does Zen Teach?

Zen teachings are profoundly different from other Buddhist practices. Many Buddhists lay emphasis on the significance of researching and comprehending the historical Buddha's teachings. Contrariwise, Zen Buddhist schools stress the importance of uninterrupted, direct experience of life. We, as practitioners of Zen, are constantly trying to comprehend the significance of life. We are taught to experience life without being distracted by often unnecessary logical thinking processes, literature, or words.

- Practice over Principle

In Zen, we are taught that we can only reach enlightenment and find our true nature while in a specific state of mind. We must practice putting ourselves into the proper form of consciousness. This is much more important that any written teachings or philosophies. Sure, scriptures will offer direction, but true enlightenment is found inside of yourself. In Zen, spending too much time on studying theories and principles will be a distraction, keeping our minds occupied with logical and practical tasks, actually preventing you from achieving enlightenment. Zen is also about getting rid of all the patterns of thinking and old ways of understanding in order to build new ways of seeing the reality and perceiving what really is around us and inside of us. The original Zen, as well as the genuine Buddha's intent, was free of almost any rituals, established practices, too many principles, etc. As one of the traditional folk stories says, when Buddha's students asked him what Buddhism was all about, he just raised a lotus flower and smiled in silence. They were confused and couldn't understand the simplicity and meaning behind what Buddha did. There was only one student who nodded and smiled. Buddha noticed that he understood and he passed all his simple teachings to him, and as the story goes, that's how Zen came into existence.

- Meditating

Meditation is one of the most important teachings in Zen. It is key to achieving the understanding. Using Zen meditation, we put ourselves into a different state of consciousness, a higher state that allows us to live an enlightened *life*, not just experience a moment of enlightenment. Zen teaches you how to quiet your active, thinking mind and concentrate on becoming truly aware. While a Zen meditative state, we are conscious of our inner self and everything around us. You become an observer of your own thoughts, not actively thinking thoughts, but being aware that they are present, without necessarily judging them, repeating them or believing in them at all. Have you ever noticed how often our own thoughts are not only not real, but also not true at all?

There are two major schools of Zen Buddhism, Soto and Rinzai, both utilize different forms of mediation.

- Luminous Mind

The idea of a luminous mind is a foundational teaching of Buddhism. There are a few slight variations, but the notion is generally the same. We must believe that the mind is luminous in order to gain understanding and to live an enlightened life. If we do not come to the realization that we have a luminous mind, we cannot properly train and develop them in order to function on a different level. The point being that our minds by nature are radiant, the thoughts and feelings that tarnish them are temporary. That means that we shouldn't be searching for the enlightenment and wisdom externally, as they are all already inside of us.

According to the traditional teachings of Zen Masters, the dominant feature of the new perception is to overcome all dualities: all that is either external or internal, the "me" and "not me," finiteness and infinity, being and non-being, illusion and reality, emptiness and fullness, necessity and randomness," so that "enlightened" and "not enlightened" or "liberated" and "not liberated" are the same thing. Zen teaches us that we shouldn't be looking for liberation in the "other worlds," as, in fact, this world is the "other world." That is the "satori" point of view, which is also known as the "perfect enlightenment," the "transcendental wisdom" (*prajnaparamita*). Does your brain hurt a little at this point? Good. Don't worry, you will ultimately understand and feel it.

We already are luminous, freed from the cycle of life and death, and already freed. Everyone already has a Buddha nature inside of them, but it is almost impossible to see and feel as our awareness is clouded and foggy. Now we just have to make our minds clear and our perception sharp enough to find this realm inside of us and connect with it.

Tarnishing thoughts and feelings will come and go. Defilements are only temporary visitors to the mind. They do not stay, nor do they permanently stain or change the mind. As long as we see it this way, believe it to be true, and analyze these things from the outside instead of actively thinking and feeling them, we can train our minds to simply observe them.

Just as a cloud momentarily blocks the sun, emotions and thoughts (when actively felt, thought, or pursued) temporarily block the radiance of the mind. We need to stop holding on to such things and let them pass by. These thoughts and feelings are comparable to darkness. We need to learn to turn on the light of our mind. When you turn on a light, darkness leaves. You cannot have it both ways, total darkness and light cannot be in a space at the same time.

Of course, the darkness will come back, but that is why we must train our minds to let go of it. We must develop our thinking to be continuously clear. We need to acquire the ability to keep the darkness out, observe it from afar. Keeping our mind luminous is the key to ultimate happiness.

- No Mind

Having no-mind, or achieving no-mindedness, is essential to living a Zen life. Too often people assume that it means to have an empty mind, when in all actuality, it is simply a state of mind that is unclouded by extensive thoughts, emotions, and feelings. When we have these things and hold onto them, we are stagnating the mind. A state of no-mind is not really still, it is constantly moving and flowing. No-mind allows us to function intuitively. It is a clean, clear, illuminating state of mind. In the Chinese understanding of Zen, we could say that it is experiencing the deepest Silence, the Primal Point of our existence - "The Road." The "No Mind" means a state that exists by itself (and which has always [forever] been there), not because of our perception, so it's not a product of our thinking and our mind.

The mind is like a mirror, reflecting the universe around us. Thoughts, feelings, and ideas are like a layer of dust coating the reflective surface of the mind. The reflection of a dirty mirror will not be clear. Yet when a mirror is dusted and clean, it shows a perfect reflection of what is in front of it. No-mind is a clean mind. This is the true state of our minds at birth. **No-mind is the perfect way to function. We must clean our minds out in order to return to this perfect state.**

What is Meditation All About?

There are quite a few ways to practice Zen Meditation. Overall, the goal of Zen Meditation is to see things for what they really are. This includes yourself and the world around you.

As we speed through life, most of us are ignorant to the fact that our logical, thinking minds and the processes of thinking that we use are the cause of much stress, hurting, and problems. **Yet, most of the time it is the type of mindset that is the actual problem, not the incident or issue that we are dealing with.**

Your real problem is not the fact that you have a problem. **The real problem is the fact that you think that you have a problem because you have the problem**.

For instance - the fact that you are not motivated to do something is not a problem. The problem is that you THINK that you have to be motivated to do something, instead of just doing it and then having it done. Tip: The willingness to do things comes with action. Don't wait until you feel like going to the gym and exercising. Start exercising right away and there's a huge possibility that you'll feel the desire to continue.

Also, your real problem is not the problem itself. It's mostly the uncertainty of its occurrence, all the waiting until it comes.

The real problem is our mind, which either escapes into the future (which doesn't exist) or creates its own visions of the past (doesn't exist either, for that matter).

Another problem is worrying that we are worried, which is making a problem out of a problem, and then making a problem that we made a problem out of the problem.

And so on. Do you get it? This madness loops itself. Regular meditation is the perfect medication for this common illness. It's the perfect training, the remedy. **All you have to do is to just stick to it on a regular basis.**

If we are constantly observing our minds through meditation, we can see what we spend (or maybe should I write: waste) our time focusing on. Usually, there is a lot of brain power used trying to get what we want in the future, longing and hanging onto what we may have lost, and figuring out why things have happened to us. We tend to compare and label everything in dualistic fashion. Is it a good thing or a bad thing? Am I making a right decision or a wrong decision? Who is in better life situation: me or my friends?

Zen Meditation allows us to observe the biases and labels that we have accumulated, and how we use them on a regular basis. Overtime, this stand-back approach to thinking and living will cause a change in the way that we process information. Indirectly, we become better people. Meditation does not directly cause us to become a better person. Instead, it enables us to study our process of living and how we understand life. One of the many results of this is that we do become a "good" person. It is a byproduct, not the goal.

Practicing Zen Meditation alters our methodology in handling thoughts, situations, and others that we come in contact with. Because of that, sooner or later, the way that we handle life will be drastically different. The way that we think and manage situations will reflect our true self, which is pure - without preconceived ideas, labels, and profiling. Our true nature does not push away things, nor cling to them. When we learn to experience life in such a manner, through meditation, that we can clearly see things for what they truly are, and appreciate them in a whole new way.

Although the details of Zen Meditation are important, do not get lost in them. They are mainly guidelines that allow you to quietly experience and discover each moment as you encounter it. Although, two main objectives should be prioritized: **to calm the mind and concentrate.**

When calming our mind, the goal is not to silence it completely. What we want to do is take a step back from *thinking* our thoughts, instead, we want to *observe* them. In order to do this we need to let go of our thoughts. Watch them pass through your brain like leaves in the wind. You will find yourself having to refocus and let go of thoughts as they come. Anytime you feel like you are *thinking* a thought instead of merely *observing* it, let it go, don't cling to it, don't continue it – you don't have to. This process will allow you to gain better control over your mind, and over time you will become better at it. Just as an athlete conditions their body, so will you be conditioning your mind. It will become easier and easier for you to harness your attention when it begins to wander off. **You will be leading your attention, instead of allowing it to lead you.** Slowly but surely, your mind will become less restless and antsy. Moodiness, emotional reactions, and feelings will pass easily.

You will also need to focus on concentrating. We can choose to concentrate on a *koan* (I will explain what it is later in this book), or just on the present moment and the feeling of being alive. When we are able to gain insight into our own minds, and experience our inner Buddha, we will be able to connect with the Buddha in all things around us.

How does One Meditate in Zen?

Zazen

Zazen is part of the foundation of Zen Buddhism. It is a Japanese term that when broken down can be loosely translated to mean sitting meditation. Although it may appear that zazen is just another simple way to calm the mind, it is actually an exceptionally effective tool that can aid us on our path to enlightenment.

This ancient meditation practice is integral to Zen Meditation. This form of meditation requires us to remain in the moment that we are currently experiencing. We are to observe thoughts, senses, and emotions, but at a distance, allowing each to just pass by like a leaf in the wind. It is the practice of not actively thinking. Zazen is simply experiencing being alive while being still.

It is important to utilize zazen without any preconceived notions of what you are trying to gain. If you practice zazen with expectations, you are definitely defeating the purpose and it will be difficult for you to simply sit. You must sit without a goal. **Zazen is known as a "non-seeking practice."** The object is to experience the very moment that you are living and feel what it is to be alive. This is what leads to enlightenment; learning about our true nature and the true nature of the world around us.

Not only does zazen help us on our path to living an enlightened life, psychologists have also found other everyday benefits! Zazen:

1) Reduces anxiety

2) Helps practitioners get rid of bad habits

3) Gives more discernment in circumstances as they arise

4) Speeds healing from certain ailments

5) Provides for more self-control to battle impulsive behavior

When you practice zazen, you should pick out a place that is quiet. You should be able to sit there for a while in silence. There should be little to no distractions going on in the place that you choose. You should not practice zazen when you are sleepy. Wear something loose and comfortable.

Here are some instructions to practice a session of zazen. It is advisable to practice with an instructor the first few times, in order to get a solid grasp of this type of meditation. It is important as zazen is such a huge part of the foundation of Zen.

1. You may need a zafu (a round meditational cushion) or a small pillow. These things are not absolutely necessary, but do aid in comfort, which in turn will improve your focus.

2. Next, choose your position. Since zazen means seated meditation, the way in which you choose to sit is very important. You can sit:

- Half Lotus: sitting with your left foot over your right thigh, and putting your right ankle/calf under your left thigh.

- Burmese: cross your legs and place both knees onto the ground. Your ankles are placed with one in front, and one behind, not over or under each other.

- Full Lotus: put the left foot on top of the right thigh and the right foot on top of the left thigh.

- Kneeling: get on your knees and allow your hips to sit on your ankles.

- Chair: you may sit in a chair with your feet on the ground (you may need a carpet) and your back completely straight. That's actually how I usually do it, but the majority of my fellow "Zen people" usually prefer the first three traditional Zen positions.

Hand positioning:

- Take your dominant hand and face it palm up. Place your other hand, palm up, on top of it. Allow your thumbs to touch. From the front your hand position should look like a circle or oval. This is known as the *cosmic mudra*. Rest your hands on your thighs or ankles depending on the seated position you choose.

- You can also wrap the first two fingers of your right hand around your thumb, forming a fist. Then put your fist on your solar plexus and cover it with your left hand, so that it covers your knuckles. Now you can adjust the angle of both arms so that it feels comfortable.

- **Note:** All of this hand positioning thing shouldn't be annoying. If you find both of these positions uncomfortable, you can either put your wrapped hands on your abdomen instead of your solar plexus or just simply put your open hands on your lap/thighs. Just use common sense.

Body Positioning:

- Your back and neck must be straight, your head will sit comfortably, and your teeth should touch but not be clenched.

3. Focus on your breath and relax your mind.

4. Count each time that you inhale and each time that you exhale. Once you reach ten, start back at one.

5. When you start to drift and begin thinking a thought, just observe it, let it go, and start focusing on the breath again. It's perfectly normal that you drift off as a beginner.

6. Now, begin counting at one.

7. Keep doing this for the amount of time that you set aside. 15 minutes is good for a beginner. Then, after a few days, you should go for 20 minutes.

8. Once you can get to ten without having to start over, count the inhale and exhale together until you reach ten. As you get better at focusing, you will be able to simply turn your attention to your breath without the need for counting. You will be able to move around in the quiet and stillness you have created. Observe your inner self and all that is around you, using all of your senses.

Although this kind of meditation may look simple, it needs some practice and patience. It's the most important element of the Zen lifestyle. When I first started, I would get irritated and uneasy almost all the time, but I had promised myself that I wouldn't stop, no matter what. I needed more than five days to slowly adjust my mind and body to stillness and emptiness. Then it started appearing easier and easier as the days went by and I still hadn't given up practicing Zazen. Since we always tend to occupy our minds with something (where "something" is so often total BS and a waste of time and energy), it's not that easy. It's like a mental detox. What's also interesting - ultimately, I started feeling this pleasant and vibrant kind of energy somewhere between my stomach and my solar plexus during my Zazen sessions. After just 20 minutes of practice, this feeling continues as I go through the day. Honestly, I don't really know what it is, but I love it. It keeps me relaxed, focused, productive and in control. I don't care if it's a placebo effect or if it's a "real thing" - it works like nothing else. From what I know, this feeling has been described numerous times by many Zen, Buddhism, Catholic and Hindu spiritual teachers, and many of my friends have experienced it as well. It may come or it may not come. Don't look specifically for this feeling. Meditation has so much to offer, that is just one of its many beneficial side effects.

Koan

Koan meditation is commonly thought of as only being used by the Rinzai School of Zen but is actually used by a wide variety of Zen practitioners. Koans are riddles, phrases, puzzles, or questions that are impossible to "solve" through rational, active, logical thinking. When we build all our judgments and replies only on what we already know, we are just limiting our horizons. When we meditate on these koans, it causes us to stop using the shallow forms of thought that we have been accustomed to using. We learn to use a different type of thought process that is unaffected by social and cultural influences. With time, that sometimes leads to the destruction of our old ineffective mind structures and creation of a new, much wider perception.

Koan Meditation is not something that Zen practitioners go at alone. Zen teachers are responsible for choosing the koan and then evaluating the answer. It is very common and understandable for Zen practitioners to come back with answers that are entirely too logical and practical.

The koan, "What is the sound of one hand?" is a great exa' koan presented to a student by a teacher. The Zen teache such riddles as a means to see where the student's mindset is, w..... *kind* of thinking the student uses in their response. The answer is not important to the teacher, it is the **kind** of answer that is important. The teacher is able to then gauge where his student is at and create the proper course of action to further them along down the road to enlightenment. Zazen is usually the next step and is normally implemented after a koan study.

Rinzai meditation commonly uses koans for meditation. Also, when practicing zazen as a Rinzai practitioner, we face each other, or the center of the room instead of the wall.

If you are interested in this type of practice and would like to know more, here I come with some useful links:

http://www.ashidakim.com/zenkoans/ - here you will find some thought-provoking koan stories.

http://www.chinapage.com/zen/koan1.html - as above

http://www.ibiblio.org/zen/cgi-bin/koan-index.pl - here you will find some of the koans I personally meditate on. Definitely recommended.

ork Meditation/Samu

Samu is any type of work done that is physical. Examples could be chores like cleaning the house or yard, preparing meals, or even chopping firewood. Practicing samu is an easy way to get more meditation in our day to day lives. It is regularly practiced in the monasteries and meditation halls, as it aids in not only keeping up the facilities, but as a way for students to maximize meditation time.

When we practice samu in our homes and in our neighborhoods it helps us to connect with our inner self while still engaging in everyday activities. It is very important to contribute to the community while practicing Zen, and samu is a great way for us to give to those around us voluntarily. We are to be generous, and what better way to show generosity than to work within the community.

Samu is a meditational practice that uses awareness. It can be done during every day activities, not just while completing chores. When you brush your teeth, you can practice Samu. Do you read the newspaper or eat a meal? Then you can easily participate in this meditational awareness.

Samu is a very simple undertaking. When you practice other Zen Meditational techniques, you give them 100 percent of your attention. In Samu, half of your attention is put into what you are doing, and the other half is devoted to being aware of the activity. It is more of a relaxed state of meditation. If we practice Samu in combination with more intense forms of meditation, we allow ourselves to remain in a constant state of meditation, from the time we wake up until we go to bed.

There is a very popular misbelief that tells us that meditation needs to be done exclusively either seated or lying down. This is not true at all. Of course, when you practice sitting meditation regularly, you will be able to be calmer and more focused while doing anything else, but as I already stated, the point of Zen is to be present at all times, all day long.

Every day we have to do certain things in order to support our lifestyles. We may work in an office, a warehouse, providing services, making products, work at home, study for a living, or teach others for a living... you get the idea. Whatever your occupation, there is work to be done. Working does not have to be looked at as a chore, or a daunting, frustrating activity. If we look at work as something that is beneficial to our lives and the lives of others, we can approach it from a different stand point. What we do effects the entire universe in some way. We are doing our part to fully participate in our life, which in turn effects not only our own life, but the lives of those around us. When we look at work from this perspective, we can see that it is essential to do whatever it is we are doing to the best of our ability.

While practicing Zen, we approach work with a different mindset. Normally when we are carrying out work that is not desirable, we tend to think about anything and everything *but* what we are doing. This lack of concentration not only results in a poor quality of work, it also ends up taking us a lot longer than it should. It makes us ineffective, unhappy, and tired. When we approach our workday using Zen Meditation, we are able to apply an enormous amount of concentration to each thing that we do. The mind is quieted, therefore allowing us to put 100% of ourselves into what we are doing.

Work can be looked forward to, as it will allow for more meditation time in your schedule. In the western world a large part of the day is spent in any given occupation. Many look at it as a waste of time, but practitioners of Zen see these hours as a way to hone and practice meditation.

Do not forget to spend a significant amount of time in sitting meditation. One does not replace the other. In fact, the better you get at sitting meditation, the easier it will be for you to quiet your mind and concentrate during work meditation (and vice versa). Practice focusing only on what you are doing, experience everything related to the job with your 5 senses, and bring your mind back to these things when it begins to stray.

What I've noticed is that even when you practice Zazen (especially as a beginner), but let your thoughts and emotions take control by not being present, alert and 100% committed to what you do in life in general, you will end up being more distracted than you should be as someone who meditates. What exactly do I mean by this?

Have you ever noticed how few people are 100% committed to what they do? Or even 90% committed?

Say that you are a student working a night shift in some fast-food restaurant where the wages are very low and the job is exhausting, repetitive and dull. You might think "This really sucks! Why do I have to be here? Being a CEO of some big fancy corporation, living in an expensive penthouse and driving a luxurious car would be really great. Or being a manager of this restaurant and just giving the orders instead of taking them." Now, what makes you think that you would be happy and have it easy as a CEO (or to begin with, even become one) if you can't even focus on frying these burgers 100% correctly and wrapping these coleslaw salads properly for your customers?

When I was working in an office (and totally hated it, to be honest), I always knew that I would never settle for that, as I have always dreamed about starting my own business, not only to earn good money, but also to earn my freedom. I know some people who just love their 9-5 jobs, but I could never adjust to that. Still, as a headhunter and an HR consultant, I tried to do my best to provide as much value as possible. Even though I didn't really care whether or not some fancy IT specialist who basically earned ten times my salary would find an even better paying job thanks to me (well, that was my mindset back then, not that I'm proud of that), I couldn't imagine not doing my best anyway, just for the sake of doing my best. If you're not 100% committed to what you do (even if it's just your chore which you have to do), then why do anything at all? Why not use that experience to learn how to discipline your mind and control your emotions, instead of just wasting your time complaining? Even though I had to battle every day with my own thoughts, I never allowed those thoughts to take control.

Now - you can't really control your thoughts and your emotions. Sorry. They just pass through you. That's why the typical Western conception of thought/emotion manipulation in order to feel more motivation, passion or enthusiasm before you do something is usually doomed for failure in the long run. You can model your thinking (by using the NLP tools, for instance), but you can't fully control it. But you can "disconnect" from your thoughts and emotions using meditation and mindfulness. You can be their witness, without believing in what you feel or paying any attention to your emotions when you don't want to. You can take action and do your own thing no matter what you feel. Here are just three simple and easy steps:

1. Accept whatever it is that you feel - let your thoughts and emotions flow through you, no matter what they are. Don't focus on controlling them.

2. Focus just on what you need to do RIGHT NOW - mantra "What is my goal RIGHT NOW."

3. JUST DO IT!

Don't manage your mind. Declare your independence instead.

When I first started working in that office and heard all these annoying songs on the radio and the boring chit-chat of my co-workers (they were mostly young moms who used to passionately discuss their babies' cute little poo, delightful coughs, awful allergies and sweet runny noses - let's just say that I could understand their genuine passion for these topics, but you see, for some reason I did not really enjoy these conversations), I told myself that it was all temporary until I gathered more experience and money to start my own business. And that was it. No more focusing on all the unnecessary thoughts. No more analyzing why I feel so bad and making a problem out of a problem. Even though I didn't like the job and knew that I didn't want to commit my life to it, I earned a lot of money for my company (even though I didn't really like my boss) and found much better jobs for many managers, IT specialists, engineers etc.

My strategy was to focus just on worrying and all the black thoughts (yes, I just wrote that) for 20 to 30 minutes before I even started my workday and get as tired with them as possible (because you have to admit that worrying about all the things you cannot change is totally exhausting). During that time, I wouldn't allow myself to think of anything but the worst things. I would passionately kill all the positivity, complaining, moaning and cursing all the way. I would probably embarrass Stephen King with all these dark visions of mine. Then after that time, only presence and productivity. I was focusing on everything but negativity, which means that instead of thinking about how I hated to be there in that cold office during the dark winter days, listening to all these dumb songs on the radio and my co-workers talking about the latest celebrity gossip, TV BS, or counting the hours till the workday's end or the days until the next weekend, I would rather focus on how my skin felt when it touched the cold plastic of a computer mouse, how my fingers clicked on the keyboard, how my back was straight and pressed against the office chair, how good my warm peppermint herbal tea tasted and how my deep breathing was making me calm and centered. I was listening to the sounds, smelling the scents and just working on my thing. Although I was doing something I didn't like, I wasn't wasting my energy. I turned my unnecessary thoughts off. I was meditating when doing my job, therefore getting the best results. I didn't even feel like I was the one sitting in that office. I was just the observer. I didn't take it personally. If you don't take things personally, you can't even complain.

Thanks to this approach, I was able to start my own business after just one year of working as a headhunter. But you need to know that I was already a Zen practitioner back then, before that . . . oh snap!

Let me show you the other side of the coin. Two years before I had even started dreaming about being a headhunter, I worked for this big online shoe company as a help-desk customer assistant. For me, that was one of the worst jobs ever. The office was nice (very dark and crowded though), people were quite friendly, but the customers . . . oh my . . . One guy even shouted out loud right into my ear that he would find me, beat me up and burn my house because the pair of shoes he received was white instead of black (which wasn't my fault at all, but that's what the job was all about - we had to repair and be sorry for what other workers higher on the ladder had already messed up). It was very stressful and exhausting, and the salary was too low to even move away from my parents, as it was my first job after I graduated. After two months of constant struggling with my thoughts *(I don't want to be here, what do all of these people want from me, how I wish I could quit this and have money to start my own business right now, please somebody answer that call, I'm sleepy, there's too many people in this office, it's dark, I'm bored, I'm this, I'm that...)*. I finally got fired, as I ended up too anxious and distracted to handle all this stress and perform well enough. The job was really bad, so it wasn't that big of a deal (although it did result in depression anyway), but had I known Zen back then, I would have been able to maintain my peace and give 100% from myself, therefore I would have been able to save more money to start my own on-line business much faster.

Basically, in all of the jobs I have ever worked, there were lots of people who would rather wander off all the time or do a careless, sloppy and totally unprofessional job, instead of accepting what is (and since there are not too many Zuckerbergs in this world, you will probably have to fulfill your dreams gradually), and committing 100% to changing that, while giving the best of themselves. That's the problem. If you can't even brush your own teeth carefully, dust the shelves with a smile on your face or wrap a stupid burger properly in a piece of paper, how do you think you will be able to successfully run a $100,000,000 company when the pressures are 1000 times stronger?

Look - what society sells us is that you need self-esteem, motivation and the right self-image to even get started with achieving your goals and being happy. Now here's the joke - you gain your self-esteem and self-confidence thanks to your effective action and the result it brings, not the other way around. You can actually start with ZERO or almost NEGATIVE self-confidence and a totally wrecked self-image (that's what I did). That's a result - not the cause. Do you lack self-worth, motivation and blah-blah-blah or what-not? Disconnect your behavior from your emotional life. That's what Zen teaches us. **You gain your self-confidence and effectiveness by facing your responsibilities EVERY DAY and overcoming the challenges that life brings you every day.** The feeling of control you then gain boosts your self-confidence/motivation and in turn, your self-confidence/motivation boosts your feeling of control. And how do you stop identifying yourself with your emotions? **Meditate.**

Meditation does not only occur when you do Zazen, sit on a park bench or listen to birds singing in the peaceful forest during a pleasant spring day. You should practice meditation no matter what you do. You should do it in your work. Be there. Be present. Be committed to what you do. Pay full attention to all those little "unimportant" things. They all do matter. Don't obsess with them, don't spend too much time on them, just pay attention and proceed carefully. As the saying goes, "The devil is in the details!" Trust me, this way your life will be much easier and much more successful.

"Don't tell me what you feel. Show me the results."

Walking Meditation/Kinhin

Kinhin is usually utilized in combination with periods of zazen. It was designed to train the practitioners to integrate the meditative awareness into everyday activities, when they're not just sitting on a cushion. When practicing kinhin, groups of practitioners walk in a circle around a room in a clockwise direction. The pace of kinhin varies from walking slowly to a jog. The pace of the walk is put into rhythm with the breath.

While walking, we hold the left hand in a fist, thumb tucked in, with the right hand covering it. The upper part of our bodies are kept in the same position that they would be during zazen. The lower part of our stomach is kept in a relaxed state, along with our neck. We tuck in our chins to keep our spines vertical and keep our stare low, at about 45 degree angle. Pure eyes are not focused on anything in particular and we may let the gaze soften.

Also be sure that you have space to walk in a fairly decent sized circle - it should be around ten feet or more in one direction. If you don't have enough space, it could also be a line instead of a circle/oval.

The form used in the steps that we take is very important. Carefully raise the left foot off of the floor, starting with your heel. Peel your foot up, from back to front, as you are inhaling a long, slow deep breath. Also focus on your breathing. Then, starting with the top of your toes, rest the left foot back onto the floor about a half foot in front of the other foot, while slowly exhaling. Now, follow the same steps for the right foot, repeating over and over as you walk silently in a circle. The length of time spent in this meditative state varies. Whenever you find yourself occupied with random thoughts or feelings, just let them be. It's okay to have them. Then just focus on your feet and your breath again.

You should be experiencing every second of every step. Notice your breath, the temperature of the air and floor, the texture of the ground under your feet. Pay attention to the shift of balance as your transfer from one foot to the other. You will need to practice walking meditation a little bit before you find your own rhythm that suits you the best. You can take baby steps or bigger strides. It can be slow or fast. You may also want to synchronize your breath with your walking. Breathe through your nose, lift one foot, inhale, and then exhale when you touch the ground. There are many Zen schools and each of them teaches walking meditation a little bit differently, but the point is to become increasingly familiar with the feeling of the breath and the touch of the ground on your feet. You can practice it in your room, your garden or somewhere on a sandy beach. You can practice alone or with your friends. With some practice and time, it will be much easier to feel present when walking to a grocery store or to work.

"Walk as if you are kissing the Earth with your feet."
— Thích Nhất Hạnh

Zen Principles

Zen, as well as Buddhism, has a total of sixteen core principles. They consist of The Three Treasures, The Three Pure Precepts, and The Ten Grave Precepts. These are principles that are applicable to both teachers, and followers. They are not so much rules as they are principals to live by. The principles are not there to keep us in line, they are there to help propel us into ourselves, allowing us to see and become one with our true nature.

The Three Treasures

The Three Treasures are principals that are the nucleus of Buddhism and Zen. They are also known as "The Three Jewels" or "The Three Refuges." It is important for Zen practitioners to "take refuge" in each one and become one with each for different purposes. Each Treasure will benefit us in a special way, aiding us in our journey to become one with our true self. Before we get to those purposes and benefits it is important to understand what it means to "take refuge" in them.

The word refuge, as it is used in conjunction with the Three Treasures, comes from the Japanese characters "kie-ei." "Kie" means to throw yourself into something without restraint and without worrying. Do not hold back and do it without reservation. "Ei" means to depend upon, have faith in, and trust. There is a game that children play that illustrates this concept perfectly. In this game, someone stands behind you. You close your eyes and fall backward, trusting that the person behind you is going to catch you. In the same way, we must rely upon the Three Treasures and throw ourselves into them without reservation.

These Three Treasures are more like vows in Zen than they are prayers or chants. They remind me of the dedication it takes to truly find and connect with my true self. They are designed to keep us focused on our goal, and remind us of the tools that we have available to keep us propelling toward it.

The Three Treasures and the vow to take refuge in them are not some magical, supernatural answer to finding your true self. They will not help you, you must help and find yourself. The "magic" in the vows, the power in their resources, comes from you. This is your journey. How committed and genuine you are will determine your ability to become one with your true self.

In order to live Zen we must:

- **Take refuge in the Buddha**

The reference to Buddha is not necessarily indicating that we throw ourselves into the historical Buddha. Rather, we can dive into his teachings and allow them to help guide us on our own paths to Buddhahood. In another sense, taking refuge in the Buddha also entails committing yourself to the goal of achieving oneness with your true nature, becoming a Buddha in your own right.

Another way of looking at this vow is that we are to commit ourselves to turning to other Buddhas for guidance and wisdom. In Zen, everything has a potential Buddha, including ourselves. This vow requires that we turn to our own inner-Buddha, as well the Buddha in everything and everyone around us for clarity and guidance.

Your meditation can be your Buddha. Your favorite professor might be your Buddha. Your wife, husband, kids, best friend or your coach can also be your Buddha. All the good books that contain precious wisdom and all of the experiences of great people accumulated through the history of our civilization definitely should be your Buddha. No man is a lonely island. You can't really achieve anything totally on your own.

- **Take refuge in the Dharma**

In the literal sense, taking refuge in the Dharma is to delve into Siddhartha Gautama's teachings in the Sutra and use them as a guide on your quest to connect with your true self. In another sense, unreservedly diving into the Dharma not only means diving into the sutra, but also the teachings of other Zen practitioners, teachers, and masters who have become one with their true selves. We can use all awakened teachings as a way to propel us closer to becoming enlightened.

There are two aspects of this treasure/jewel. In Sanskrit, Dharma means "truth." This refuge represents both the actual truth of teachings and the comprehension, acceptance, and application of these truths. When we use them in our everyday lives to solve problems and to connect with or find our true self, we are taking refuge in the Dharma.

- **Take refuge in the Sangha**

The vow to take refuge in the Sangha means to surround yourself with a community or assembly of people who follow Zen teachings. These are people who have either awakened and connected with their true self, or are striving to.

My mother always said, "You are who you hang around," and that is the meaning behind this vow in a nutshell. We need to surround ourselves with people who have attained, or are on their way to achieving, like-minded goals. In this case, we are trying to become one with our true self. In order to strengthen our resolve and stay on the path to enlightenment, we should keep company with people who will advise, encourage, support, and be a good example. We should choose a solid group of people to hang around who practice and follow the teachings of Zen.

The Three Pure Precepts

These three guidelines are simple concepts that are powerfully profound to followers of Zen Buddhism. There are varying translations of these precepts, but they all have the same underlying principles:

1) Do not do anything evil.

   Do not bring harm to anyone, or anything, including all things in the universe. Do not engage in any behavior or indulge in any thought brought on by the Three Root Poisons: greed, anger, and ignorance.

2) Only do good things.

Let your actions reflect your new and awakened spirit, your true self. Thoughts and behaviors that are free of the Three Root Poisons are considered good. Morality and enlightenment go hand in hand.

3) Help good things to happen to other people.

Do everything in your power to give others a chance to find and show their true self. Once you are on the path to enlightenment, or living an enlightened life, it will cause you to pour that over into others' lives.

The Ten Grave Precepts

These all lead us to become our true selves. If you want to live a life of uprightness and honor, follow these precepts. You will be happier.

1) Do not murder. Do not persuade or inspire other people to kill.

2) Do not steal. Do not condone or promote stealing by others.

3) Do not misuse sex in any way.

4) Do not say false things or encourage others to do so.

5) Refrain from drinking alcohol or taking other drugs.

6) Do not speak about things that others do wrong or their faults.

7) Do not speak highly of yourself and put down others.

8) Do not be ungenerous.

9) Do not hold on to anger or encourage others to indulge in anger.

10) Do not slander the Triple Jewel: the Buddha, the Dharma, or the Sangha.

The Ten Grave Precepts can be interpreted in three different ways: literally, figuratively, and practically. For example, a literal translation of number one would be not to kill anyone or any living creature. Practically speaking, you could choose to go so far as to sweep your walkway to ensure that you will not step on any bugs. Figuratively, you would need to make sure that you do not kill anything including someone's hopes and dreams by saying discouraging things.

Although the Ten Grave Precepts may seem outdated or impractical in our modern western culture, they are anything but. The first five precepts are especially important for those of us practicing Zen in the modern world. They have many practical applications and will enhance your path to enlightenment, add to your already enlightened life, and benefit the world around you. How so? Good question! Here are a few of the many ways that these precepts apply to western culture:

1. Do not murder.

Yes, traditionally, we are taught that killing is wrong. Yet, if we dig a little bit deeper and look at killing and murdering with open eyes, we can see that this precept needs to be fully embraced and practiced by westerners. In the West, we have been programmed to see ourselves as independent, self-governing individuals, detached from others. This is a far-fetched notion when viewing life from a Zen perspective.

We are all interconnected. The choices of one effect the life of another. We are all Buddha. Therefore, in everything that we do we must consider what effect our choices and decisions will have on the people and things around us. In Zen, there is no autonomy.

There is a common unawareness in western culture that breaking the first precept in your mind is sometimes just as harmful as physically doing it. It is very common for us as society to allow our youth to play violent games and watch brutal movies. Have you ever noticed that in our strange Western culture, nudity is always perceived as something far more disturbing, "wrong" and definitely less acceptable on TV during the day (and everyday life in general) than brutal violence? We basically think that a pair of women's breasts or a scene where two people kiss and touch each other causes more harm to kids and teenagers than graphic scenes of murder, torture and blood all over the walls, so popular in movies, cartoons, comic books, games, etc. What's wrong with this picture? From playing cowboys and Indians, to playing video games where killing is common place, our culture is programming and desensitizing us to be somewhat numb to these horrors.

Now, I'm not saying that anyone who plays video games that include killing and violence will automatically become a psychopath or unhappy person, or that boys should stop playing cops and thieves and choose dolls instead. No. Actually I used to play some really violent games back in the '90s and I still like to watch a good thriller or a horror movie once in a while (not to mention a good thriller book on a long rainy evening)! But it's all about balance and harmony. If you drink a small amount of strong alcohol once every few weeks, nothing bad will happen and it can even be healthy. If you drink yourself away on a daily basis, it will ruin both your health and your emotions.

The same goes for all the information you feed your brain with. If you provide it with violence, horror, aggressive music and graphic movies all the time, believe it or not, it will ultimately change you (especially if you're young, but not only the young people). It will kill your clarity and awareness. When I was a teenager I used to get extremely pissed off whenever my parents told me to "turn off that terrifying aggressive music" and "stop playing these obnoxious violent stupid games." (Were the games stupid? Not really - I've learned a lot from many of them. Violent? You bet). Of course, I never really listened to my parents, believing that they just came from a different planet. When I started reading more about Buddhism and Zen a few years later, I discovered that they were right. Maybe not entirely, as they were playing the typical "worried parents" role during those days and they would probably be glad to see me studying 23 hours a day and drinking cod-liver oil every ten minutes back then, but they had the right thoughts. The point is that you have to be extremely careful about what you are feeding your brain with. I have always been a heavy metal and rock music fan and that will never change, because I love the sound and I've grown up on it, but I discovered that listening to all this stuff on a daily basis, a few hours a day, has the ability to make me aggressive, distracted and emotionally unstable. As much as I still love this kind of music and still go to concerts sometimes, I have to admit that listening to all these loud songs about death, wars, demons, dragon slayers, blood, unrequited love and taking drugs all the time does not really help me to focus and be a calm person. Now many people can say that it's just typical BS (especially teenagers, I'd say the same if I still was one), but you can just start listening to something calm and steady for a few weeks and see what happens with your ability to focus, study or do your work without distractions and how your emotional rollercoaster will significantly diminish (if you have them). And it doesn't just apply to aggressive rock or metal music. What good lyrics do in general is that they take us on an intensive emotional trip, with highs and lows. After we stop listening, we feel like we just experienced catharsis, but so often it's just kind of an emotional hangover. I actually used to be a music addict (especially since I play guitar and have my own little semi-pro recording studio in my room). I would start listening to my favorite tracks right after waking up and continue until late at night - on loudspeakers, headphones, mobile, in the kitchen, in the bathroom, everywhere. That would really keep me from doing all the tasks I wanted to complete and it also caused many strange emotional responses. I was extremely easy to irritate, as I had listened to songs about so many serious human issues during these days. I'm still a little bit of a music junky, but thanks to meditation and Zen I have learned how to appreciate silence and emptiness, which has skyrocketed my productivity and emotional steadiness. Looking for music that would rather calm me down and support my goals instead of feeding me with excessive drama, I've also greatly broadened my musical horizons and started listening to electronic music (ambient, electronica and IDM, mainly), folk music (Tibetan chants for example) and also classical, jazz and instrumental music in general, which really changed my perception and helped me produce much better recordings. So you see, something that you totally love can also kill your right perception, your productivity, and your peace.

But that's just one example. As an amateur musician I could write a lot about it, but you can kill your good mood, clarity and perception in many other ways.

How we as Westerners usually kill our peace, clarity of mind and intent and stillness is simple and typical - we don't know how to use TV, radio, Internet and other media. (By the way - check this website - http://unplugthetv.com/ - it shows you a short movie that you should watch instead of mindless TV watching - the content is not always the best, but anyways, nice shot). We don't control ourselves, we just drift. So often we feel empty and try to fill this vast space with social websites (also known as "let's spy on my friends, see how they are doing", get depressed that they are doing better - because all these pictures say so), watching TV series ("I'll just watch this one short episode" . . . but then there's always five more coming), listening to celebrity gossip (because why handle your own life and feel better? Let's just allow *Justin Belieber's* new teenage girlfriend or *Berlin Hilton's* new palace to be more important). We, as a society in general, don't even know how to use smartphones. Go into any club or take a bus ride - usually more than half of these people will be playing with their new super-duper-fancy *Pear J-Phone* or *Heissung Andromeda* phone, browsing through their *appearance-book* walls for the 20th time that day, looking as smart as zombies, even if they are out together with their friends, family or a partner. Honestly, a coma looks more fun. That's how social meetings look nowadays.

The truth is (OK, this is my personal opinion, don't shoot me if you work for the media sector) - more than 95% of what they show you on TV, play on the radio or what people clutter their minds with when browsing popular portals on the Internet is just t-o-t-a-l sewage. It is crap, pure BS. It is such a big waste of energy and time, and an endless black hole where all the clarity of mind and calm goes and disappears forever.

Do you want to truly be happy? CUT – IT – OFF!

Do you know how I use my smartphone?

1) I sometimes call my friends and family.

2) I sometimes write text messages.

3) I play brain games every day for 20 minutes to improve my speed and develop new ways of thinking.

That's it. No *appearance-book*. No reading about *Ewan McKrugor's* new wife. No watching *Christiana Acoolera-Whatever* new big breast implants (OK, OK... I know the "real names", I just didn't have anyone in particular on my mind when writing this – I'm referring to the "celebrities' world" and "hype products" in general). No endless chats with my "besties" about nothing at all and more. I don't know the newest top chart "super hits." I don't know who won the last big game. I have no idea who killed whom in the latest *Game of Fancy Chairs*. I-DON'T-CARE-AT-ALL. I just follow two funny comedy series as they cheer me up and I have been watching them for more than ten years now, so you can call me a faithful fan. It's all about two short episodes a week when I want to relax before hitting the bed. But as the statistics say, the average American spends F-I-V-E hours a day watching TV! And this doesn't mention the time spent on the Internet (either on computers, tablets or smartphones) and listening to all the crap they usually play and tell you on the radios.

Is Zen about being ignorant? If you ask me, it's about selective ignorance. Life is short, whether we like it or not. Our minds were never designed to assimilate even 1/50 of all the information we receive every day, especially given that most of it is usually total junk.

Is it as simple as that - if you want your mind to be calm, happy and smart, you need to feed it with calm, happy and smart content. When you want your emotions to support you, you need support your emotional system. If you want to escape the impression that your life is flowing through your fingers, you need to stop wasting your time. If you want to focus and succeed, then you have to save as much time as possible and start using it effectively.

Don't murder your time. Don't murder your mind.

Also, while it is easy to get stuck on the murdering of fellow humans when we think of the First Precept, we as westerners lose sight of the fact that murdering any life on the planet is wrong. Practicing Zen Buddhism and following this precept will widen the narrow view that modern culture takes on the act of killing. Meditation allows us to conceptualize reality on another level. This is a must do considering that our planet is dying and we are only perpetuating the destruction. Broadening our view of life and living will enable us to take a step back and come up with solutions for all of the harm we have done to our planet. Using Buddhist wisdom, we can more easily see ourselves as part of "the big picture" instead of independent beings, and then begin to analyze how we can fix this world collectively.

As I write this, the Amazon Rainforest, also known as the "Lungs of Earth," is being destroyed at a terrifying pace. There's more than 90 animal species globally that are either endangered or a few inches from dying out totally and forever, including the bees. Without them our ecosystem will be changed irreversibly, as well as our lives. I won't even mention the plants, coral reefs (they will soon be gone), etc. Big American, Canadian and European corporations are corrupting politicians and lawyers in Africa, South and Middle America, poisoning the soil with oil, industrial toxic waste, totally ignoring the law and hurting people, both directly and indirectly. We are fishing more fish and seafood than the oceans can handle, so that in a near future there might be no more tuna and many other fish. The ozone layer is widening and the glaciers are melting. The water levels are rising. The rain is acidic and the diseases of our civilization are spreading, and that's just the tip of the iceberg.

Our planet is slowly dying, but they won't tell you that on TV, because who really cares when you can watch such prominent and intelligent shows as "Date my Son" or "Make Out With My Mum," "See All These Fancy Villas and Countless Insanely Expensive Cars of Mine I Don't Even Drive When There Are Children Starving and Dying in Africa (But Who Cares?)," "See My SWAG Dude, LOL, ROTFL LOL2," "Another Absolutely Unbiased And Totally Reliable World News to Make You Feel Scared, Anxious and Thinking That Everyone and Everything Outside the U.S. Wants to Kill You" and all the other great stuff that you should definitely be up to date with. You also shouldn't forget about the numerous cat pictures and fail movies on the Internet. And the appearance-book! Yay - likes, likes, gimme more likes! Because it's so insanely important what all the other people think of you! And . . . oh, wait, there's my smartphone ringing . . .

. . . So should you just sit and cry and feel bad about what we do to our planet? Should you be paranoid? No, but who would really care about the Earth, controlling politicians' actions and the global economy when people voluntarily prefer to fill their minds with all this rotting garbage on a daily basis? It's their drug that they demand. They choose to kill their minds, their awareness and their happiness every day. They literally choose to live as dull zombies. Talk about the importance of spiritual development. Look around you. We don't even usually know how to form proper social relationships anymore. Boys don't know how to talk to girls. They are AFRAID OF GIRLS! They prefer porn. Girls don't know how to be girls. Adult men act like stupid spoiled kids or dumb pseudo-Alpha jerks. Women act like dizzy cows and fake plastic dolls (don't get me wrong here, I'm just showing you my personal point of view regarding human relations in our "modern" Western society). We prefer typing on appearance-book (where we have thousands of "friends," but don't really know anyone) than meeting real people and talking. Strong family bonds barely exist. Nothing's ever going to change for the better if we don't quit killing our consciousness, awareness and clarity of mind. It will just get worse and worse and then we will probably end up like in this movie "Idiocracy" (funny or not, but the intro was scarily accurate), or even worst. On this note, I recommend that you Google and read about "The Mouse Utopia Experiment." Eye-opening.

The act of following the Buddhist Precepts helps us to cleanse our minds. In Buddhism, goodness and wisdom flows from a clean mind. Morality is a result of a purified mind. Our actions reflect how we think, and if we act using purified minds, our actions will also be pure by nature. Our actions will reflect our enlightened state. Enlightened individuals see the universe as a whole, even viewing everything in our environment as alive. Therefore, we must take care to not cause harm to our world. We should refrain from killing anything in our water, or bringing harm to anything due to our collective pollution of the water. This is also applicable to the air and the soil. We should refrain from killing bugs, animals, tiny organisms, birds, plants and start thinking deeply about the consequences of our choices... you get the idea.

2. Do not steal.

Stealing, by definition, is taking something that does not belong to you. Not only does this precept instruct us to not take *things* that do not belong to us, it also includes taking advantage of people. When we take advantage of others, we are gaining something that is not given freely to us. This type of thievery includes financial gain, products, services and even physical labor.

In our culture, it can be very difficult to figure out who you may be stealing from. For instance, if you are buying clothes that were made in a sweatshop in Bangladesh, you are technically "stealing." The companies employing the people making the clothes are usually taking direct advantage of their labor. These large companies force laborers to work fourteen-fifteen (or more) hours a day and pay them close to nothing. You are supporting that by purchasing the clothes. Following the Second Precept, you should refrain from this type of thievery, for the good of all. Modern life complicates things that used to be so easy. By using ancient Buddhist wisdom, we can simplify things. We can use the precepts to uncomplicated the complexities of modern life.

You can also steal other people's good feelings and emotions by pointless criticizing, trolling or negativity. There's a saying that goes, "Weak people revenge, strong people forgive, intelligent people ignore." If someone has stepped on your toes, the best thing that you can do for your own good is to forgive that person. That might be difficult, but you can't do anything better than trying, as "holding on to anger is like grasping a hot coal with the intent of throwing it at someone else; you are the one who gets burned." (Fun fact: Buddha probably never said that, and it's just a simplified quote from Visuddhimagga IX, 23, but it's still very wise). Whenever you cling onto anger and hatred, it just destroys your own clarity of judgment, spoils your own good behavior and ultimately makes you miserable. You can also steal by not understanding that people have their own problems, and being the person that complains and criticizes everything all the time is just emotional thievery. Also, stop correcting people all the time, preaching to them and commenting on all the subjects you have no idea about. Stop being a part-time all-purpose expert on everything. You don't have to be RIGHT all the time, chillax. Stop trolling the Internet forums and message boards, giving 1-stars and down-voting everything that doesn't go with your vision of reality (tip: your vision might be wrong). Stop bringing people down just because you feel miserable. So often we just CHOOSE to feel bad. Do you know why? No one really cares about the ones who feel good. No one will come to you, hug you and pay so much attention to you if you are content, successful and just alright (unless it's hyper-success or popularity, but that's another thing). But when you're sad and feel bad? Then you might deserve a pat on your back, a hug, an encouraging word, and all these countless questions about how you feel and where your life is going. It's ironic how often we don't really want to feel good and succeed. We want to attract attention instead. We want other people to be sorry for us. We want to be the CENTER of our world, no matter if happy or not. That's just thievery. You steal other people's time, their good emotions and their energy just to feed your vain ego and to so often make yourself and the people around you even more miserable. Don't do that! Don't choose the negativity and don't be the toxic and bitter person. Don't steal that way. Also, don't steal people's dreams just to tell them "that won't ever go well" or "it's impossible, you can't do that," just because you don't have the bravery to try it yourself or you don't think it is "right." Provide other people with a smile, good energy and a good word and you will be happy. There's no need to steal at all, it just wrecks your own reality.

3. Do not misuse sex.

In the modern, western world, we have to look at this precept a bit differently than how it was traditionally adhered to. By tradition, monks are celibate. Also, this precept generally guided practitioners to follow the cultural standards for marriage. Yet today, the institution of marriage is a shell of what it used to be.

In many modern cultures, it is common for people to be monogamous with different partners over their lifetime and never marry. Children born out of wedlock is such a common occurrence nowadays that people hardly bat an eye to it. Divorces happen so often it makes some people wonder what the point of getting married is in the first place.

People these days are very often addicted to pornography, no matter if they have sexual partners or not. It also kills clarity and awareness and makes them distracted. People also become totally obsessed about sex and feeding their egos, making it the number 1 goal of all goals and often hurting others just to get their pleasure. You can actually have a whole lot of pleasure and be even more miserable and unhappy, but I will expand on this later in this book. There are lots of people who have had tons of sexual partners and are more unhappy and depressed, as they don't know how to form meaningful relationships anymore or how to truly open themselves to others. On the other hand, there are as well people who are afraid of others, therefore living lonely lives of despair, devoid of real emotions, warmth and all the proximity and intimacy they need. That's because they don't have any insight into their lives, they don't know who they are and what they really want. There is no balance in their lives. They let the porn business, TV, media, friends, newspapers, magazines, gurus and their bad emotions dictate their actions. They just drift.

All of these things have serious effects on our collective consciousness. They also carry serious repercussions. STDs are almost at epidemic proportions. Children from broken homes sometimes develop serious emotional issues which can result in delinquency or even substance abuse. Broken homes have also led to financial peril for many families. This has a terrible effect on the economy. And so the vicious circle goes.

4. Do not say false things.

This precept is not simply speaking about lying. It also covers saying mean things that would cause someone else pain and manipulating people. Anything that is not pure in nature we should not be said. Our words should be beneficial to ourselves as well as the others and true.

When we practice Zen, we are trying to achieve complete honesty with ourselves. When we are true to ourselves then and only then can we be trusted to be true to others. In this day and age it is common for people to be dishonest and deceptive. Many people justify it, so long as no law is broken.

This type of deceit is present from the bottom to the top of the food chain. People lie or change their appearance, lie on their resumes, and pretend to be someone else on the web. Corporations falsify documents, scientific data, and even lie about their finances. Technology has advanced so much that it makes it easy to fool others.

When I was in high school I desperately needed some extra money to take this hitchhiking trip down south with my friends. One of them helped me find a job where we sold cheap perfumes. That was a canvassing job. We were given products that were originally bought for as little as a few cents from various Chinese suppliers and then were trained to sell them for as much as possible. The business model was quite ordinary, but we were taught how to manipulate people through many behavioral psychology and sales tricks, and it actually worked. The money was very good for me as a teenager (it was actually pretty good overall, if someone was motivated), and I was getting closer and closer to my financial goal, and to my dream trip... until the time I sold a three-pack of these smelly cheap perfumes to an old woman who barely could pay her bills. I just used all these techniques they taught us to successfully close the deal and then moved to a few another apartments. After a little more than an hour, the woman approached me at the staircase and asked me to give her the money back. She told me that because of all this fancy talk we used on people, she stopped thinking for a moment, but then her husband returned home and she remembered that they had more bills to pay than she thought, and she had to buy her medicine for her back pains. At some point she almost started crying. I felt totally bad. Our boss was driving with us and controlling our sales, counting the money every few hours and collecting the money. At that point the money was already counted and taken away from us, so I couldn't give it back to her. I even considered giving the money back from my own pocket, but I didn't have any. That day I wasn't able to sell anything else. I went home and started thinking about my goal and all of the shady practices we used to apply to sell these cheap, low-quality perfumes to people who didn't even need them. I went to that job two more times, then I quit. I never went on this hitchhiking trip down south with my friends, but I gained a clean conscious. I wasn't able to earn this kind of money even some time after graduation, but still, earning it just didn't feel right. The sense of just decision and congruence with my own standards and values turned out to be far more important, purifying and relieving than spending two weeks with my friends on some hot beach, under a palm tree, spending money that I earned by selling a heavily overpriced low-quality product. I gathered a group of friends and we went to a lakeside cottage somewhere in the wild for a few days instead. And I have never really regretted this decision. Especially when I later found out that one of my friends had gotten beaten up by some angry client on steroids who had also decided that he wanted his money back after the "magic spell" had stopped working.

Remember - you can deceive other people, but you can never deceive yourself and your conscience - at least not for too long, and those who "can" always end up miserable.

5. Refrain from drinking alcohol or taking other drugs.

Alcohol and drugs inhibit us. They cloud our minds, impair our judgment, produce unnatural feelings and emotions, and keep us from being who we truly are. It is hard enough to stop thinking, find your true self, and live an enlightened life because of the social and cultural influences that we are bombarded with during the course of our lifetime. It is difficult to find out who we truly are and experience life the way that it should be thanks to many events in our lives that have caused us emotional trauma. Why should we make it more difficult and alter our minds further, intentionally? In order to live an enlightened life we need to purify our minds in order to be able to function with a clear conscious.

Drugs and alcohol will not only provide you with a thick layer of brain fog, they will also lower you inhibitions and cloud your moral judgment. In fact, partaking in such substances may very well cause a lapse in judgment leading to the breaking of other important precepts.

I once committed myself to this little experiment, to stop drinking for one year. Yes, 365 days, no alcohol at all. Well, I'm still alive, and the results were amazing. The hard part was that in our culture alcohol is inextricably linked with to so many social events - birthdays, weddings and so on - that it was also a great test for my assertiveness, as my friends would always encourage me to drink with them. After a few weeks they started asking me all these strange questions - "dude, are you on rehab?" "Did you become a priest?" "Have you been through a trauma?" and so on. It was really hard to explain that I just wanted to see what happens when you quit alcohol for one year as I have always been very inquisitive. Anyway, I did it and even though I like to have a beer sometimes, I'm really proud that I had decided to do that and achieved my goal and I'd like to recommend this kind of challenge to everyone as it has really improved my self-confidence when it comes to being an achiever. Apart from that, I saw some really interesting effects:

-I was able to go to a barbecue or a club party and talk to people normally while feeling totally cool without a glass or a bottle of alcohol in my hand.

-I was more energized, it was MUCH easier to wake up in the morning (I would begin every day at 6 a.m., sometimes earlier, and feel like a newborn even after sleeping for just six hours - actually I still keep this habit even though I don't usually really have to wake up in the morning.)

-My results at gym were much better. I gained muscle faster, I regenerated faster and I had more power and stamina to lift heavy weights.

-I stopped losing my focus and going about my days in a "walking daze." The "brain fog" disappeared.

-I felt the urge to eat clean and healthy.

-I was more stable emotionally.

These days, I like to have my glass of bourbon on ice once every few weeks or a bottle of a decent beer, but I have stopped heavy drinking (especially at parties) for good and I have never regretted this decision. When you don't drink yourself away too frequently, it is MUCH easier to meditate and maintain a balanced lifestyle on a daily basis.

This precept, in modern western culture, should not only include illegal drugs and alcohol, but the legal ones as well. Prescription drug abuse is a growing problem, and when these substances are abused they carry the same dangers as the illegal drugs. Not to mention the fact that many prescription drugs are a quick fix for emotional problems that can keep us from living an enlightened life. We need to address these issues in order to connect with our true nature, not numb ourselves or just put on a Band-Aid. Also, the abuse of legal substances such as caffeine and nicotine alter our thinking processes as well. We cannot fully connect with our Buddha nature with so many things in the way. Basically, anything that affects your awareness and perception of reality will make it much harder for you to connect with your true self. For example, Marijuana and many other "soft" drugs such as LSD or DMT, have been strongly connected to eastern "spiritual" style in the minds of some people (especially young people who are still looking for their path and meaning in life), yet it's just a big cliché and I would not recommend that.

Does that mean that you can't meditate and find your true self while using these substances? You probably can, but you **don't need**

them at all and in the long run you will really be able to meditate and focus much better without any awareness-changing substances. It's like all of these people who need to have a few beers to be able to start a conversation with a woman or a gentleman during parties. Are they really self-confident or socially aware when they need alcohol to meet someone? I wouldn't say so. So you may have some interesting insights and experiences while trying these substances, but if you can't have them on a regular basis while being a "natural" meditation practitioner, it's worthless and can even prove detrimental to your clarity of mind and the ability to focus and meditate. There are also some people who try to solve their problems with these substances. That's like drowning your problems in alcohol - it will just destroy you, make you feel bad, emotionally withdrawn, empty and confused. Zen is about experiencing, not about escaping from the bad feelings and just clinging to the good emotions. You can detach from these feelings as a Zen practitioner, but you can't really "escape" from them as such. In fact, even such mundane substances as caffeine affect your awareness and how your brain works, in a bad way. If you are a caffeine addict (lots of people are these days), it will be a little bit harder for you to be a good Zen practitioner than it will be for all these people who don't need any external substances to feel awake (deep meditation makes you feel awake). In fact, caffeine doesn't really work, even though you might be sure it does. It just gives you a quick artificial up-lift, then you fall down and feel even sleepier. I recommend that you read some scientific research about coffee and switch to a good green tea instead (in moderation, too)! Anyway, remember, **the less external chemicals put into your**

body and mind, the better. All this input affects your neurobiology. Stay natural! You will be surprised how clear your mind can become without all this stuff.

Chapter 3: Living Zen

In order to live Zen, we must experience every moment fully while engaged in it. This concept seems so simple, yet it had a profound effect on my entire life. I know that it will change yours as well. Such a seemingly simple idea, living every moment, will alter and better your life in ways you might have never thought.

Most of us do not start down a path of enlightenment and Zen living to become a better person, but thankfully it is definitely a byproduct of the journey as you feel happier and more fulfilled. When you learn to act with your newfound clear mind, you will find that every area of your life will improve. Shedding fear, old hurt and negative emotional responses will allow you to act and react in the most natural way possible. You will be able to live without too much thinking, and there is nothing more freeing or liberating. Here are 3 ways that you will indirectly be a better person in your everyday Zen practice:

1. You will not worry.

If we are living in the now, experiencing this very moment, occurring right now, there is no way that we can worry. When you focus solely on what is actually happening, you cannot worry. Worrying is so common in this day and age that often times we do not even realize that we are doing it. The effects of worry in our lives are too numerous to count. If we get rid of it, we will be happy. If we look at this very second, the one we are experiencing right now, nothing is usually wrong. It's just our tiresome never-ending train of thoughts, all these negative voices in our heads and bad emotions. By eliminating worry from our lives we are able to look at the good things we have going on; we notice and can appreciate the amazing life that we are living. Removing worry from our mind causes a huge change in perspective.

A few years ago I felt really anxious and decided to read my own diary. That was a huge .doc document I had been creating for a few years then. It took me all day and a lion's share of the night to go through it, but the insight I made was priceless. When I first started that diary I was a depressed, excessively anxious 21-year-old boy. I was really lost in my own life. At the beginning, the diary served as an emotional drain. It was a log where I used to transfer all my nightmares, black visions, fears, insecurities and worst memories. I figured out that every time I confessed all these things to my friends and people close to me, it just would make me feel even worse (like a big walking failure who can't even handle his own emotions and life), so I decided to write about all these things instead and it proved helpful (there are actually numerous scientific researches proving that writing one's emotions down is much more helpful than talking about them with a friend). But do you know what I found out after a few years, when I finally decided to read this diary?

More than 99% of my fears and worst expectations NEVER BECAME REALITY. The 1% that came true was usually not even a quarter as scary and bad as I had thought it would be, and all of these things and their consequences were usually easy to repair and overcome.

The handsome, sporty and well-dressed guy, always surrounded by a group of irresistibly attractive women, hitting on the girl I totally liked and dated, turned out to be her homosexual friend she liked to shop for clothes with. The "hater" professor supposed to bail almost every student on the year turned out to actually like me. The last exams on the university turned out to be ten times easier than I thought and I earned an "A" on my graduation degree. I finally went to the gym and no one laughed at my weak, skinny body and actually some of these big guys wanted to help me for free. I didn't have stomach cancer and the gluten allergy test turned out to be negative. My neck concussion disappeared after just few a weeks and I never had to go to the hospital. My girlfriend never met anyone she liked better than me, even though we were having a long-distance relationship for two months while she was in Wales . . . and so the list goes . . . on and on.

All this time I spent on worrying, all these MS WORD pages cluttered with digital curses, a negative vision of the world and black predictions about my future . . . all this fear I decided to let in my mind, all these sleepless nights, all this frustration - all for nothing. Such a big waste of time and energy. And we all do that. We worry about this, that, now, then, her, him, them and what not, but 99% of our thoughts are just totally useless utter nonsense, repeated so many times in our heads, that we start believing the lie. It's a biased, all-black-painted version of reality. Don't fall for that!

Another interesting concept for you - life is just a game. Buddhism teaches us than nothing is truly real and this world is an illusion of our own perception, as we are too limited to fully see the world as it is. So the game is played both externally and internally - inside of you. Let's say that your better side plays with your worst side. Instead of resisting and fighting, you have to make the better side win, at the same time realizing that the worst side will do everything to be at the top. That means acceptance of all the things happening inside of you and not "buying" your own excuses, stories, bad trips and black visions. In short - the point being that you can't even treat yourself personally and seriously. You shouldn't believe the majority of your thoughts.

2. You will begin to make better choices.

When our decision making is not fueled by fear, events of the past, or the opinions of others, it becomes much easier to make beneficial decisions. Your choices will reflect your true nature. You will be able to use the wisdom that you have gained to make decisions that will benefit you and those around you. The more often that you make great decisions on your own, the more confident you will be. The decisions you make show others your character. You will also see that when making big decisions in your life, you have to take full responsibility for the outcome and the process; doing so feels great. Before I started my journey with Buddhism and Zen, I always needed "feedback" from my friends - probably to be able to blame them in my own mind in case something went wrong, so I could therefore feel more secure - is the track I just recorded good enough? Does it sound right and full-dimensional? (Of course, you don't even know how to compose a five-second cell-phone ring jingle using the "Automatic Single-Click No-Effort Music Super Fool-Proof Software" and you listen to your music on laptop loudspeakers, but I definitely need to know your valuable pro opinion!). Is the girl I am dating now pretty enough and do you think that she's smart and good for me? (Even though I have never liked any of your girlfriends and I think they were all as close to deep thinking and emotional maturity as the Pope is to black rap). Do you think that I should quit my job and go on this backpacking trip to Bolivia? (Of course, you have never had any job longer than one week and never went outside of the U.S., but please, tell me how to proceed)? You get this. Although feedback from an experienced person can sometimes be a good thing, we so often think that we need advice from literally everyone in our social circle. ("No! Don't quit the job you hate so much and never go on that trip! It's so immature and dangerous . . . and now let me just finish my fifth beer and that joint, go back to my mom's apartment and play *World of Wimpcraft* all night long"), which makes our judgments biased and our choices much worse. We don't usually trust ourselves. Why do you think that you can't decide what is good for you on your own? The deep self-insight that comes from regular meditation will help you here - a lot.

3. You will be more positive.

When we live a Zen lifestyle, we are automatically forced into thinking more positively. How so? Well, when we remove worry, labels, judgments, negative speech and thinking, lying, and many other things that do not coincide with Zen, we find that what we are left with is a positive mindset. When you remove things that are not currently happening from clouding your thinking, you will naturally be able to think in a much more optimistic way. The optimistic state of mind is the only one that really drives the upwards spiral of success. When you start anything with a negative state of mind, you will soon become your own worst enemy, and even if you were born just to do what you just planned, your own doubts and lack of motivation will kill your journey, sooner or later. Zen lifestyle is greatly helpful when it comes to personal success, which has been known for a long time in big, successful companies, and has been used in such practices as Kaizen and other similar coaching and continuous-improvement systems.

How to Slow Down

We, as westerners, are sucked into an idea that we are not being productive if we are not working at a fast pace. Yet, when we look at life from this perspective, we will most likely feel disappointed on a regular basis. We will be constantly pushing ourselves to the max, focusing on what we need to do or what we haven't done. This type of outlook is completely counterproductive for those practicing Zen. If we are constantly worried about what we have to do or what we didn't do, we cannot delve completely in to what we *are doing*. We have to remember that life is about the journey, it is not about the finish-line. In Zen, we strive to truly experience every single moment. What better way to be able to do so then by taking our time?

I will share with you some tips that have allowed me to slow down my pace and get the most out of a Zen lifestyle:

- Set your pace first thing in the morning. If you start out slow it is easier to continue in that mode all day, rather than starting out like a bat out of hell and then committing yourself to slow down. Start off your mornings by (for example):

    1. Going for a walk or run.

    2. Indulging in a session of yoga.

    3. Practicing some sitting meditation.

    4. Taking a relaxing bath.

    5. Reading a book.

By beginning your day with a slow pace, you are setting the tone for the rest of the day. You will be moving slower and thinking slower allowing you to indulge in and maybe even enjoy every task you undertake. Slowing down and living each day at a slower place helps me to feel like my productivity levels are through the roof, despite the fact that I have not gotten a million things "done". Life is about quality, not quantity.

How to slow down your mornings:

- Tabulate a list of 7 different ideas for starting off your morning. Pick activities that will boost your health and positivity. I picked:

-stretching and pushups session,

-30 minute intense bicycle ride to the seafront and back home,

-quick run to a swimming pool where I spend 30 minutes on intensive swimming session,

-jumping on a rebounder, 15 minutes session,

-healthy breakfast with my girlfriend on a balcony,

-waking up at 5 A.M, drinking lemon juice, then carefully completing all these tasks that have needed completion for a long time, during the first hour, before the breakfast.

-dancing and karaoke session on Sundays ☺

Moreover, I start every day with a loud reading of my own life-goals and goals for a present month.

Now, come up your own list and use a different one of these every day to start your morning off right.

Besides that:
- Make sure that you are getting enough sleep. You can go to bed earlier. You can get up earlier. Choose what will work best for you, allowing you to feel energized so that you can give your day 100%.

- At first, you will need to put extra effort into moving and living slowly. Put active attention into remaining calm and peaceful. Every time you have to redirect your thinking back to your slow pace and tranquility, remember that you are strengthening and training your mind to function this way. That's one of the differences between people and animals. We can train ourselves.

Mindfulness on Steroids

Let me now show you how to super-boost your presence.

The basic tool of people who do great in the situations of extreme uncertainty, pressure, chaos and danger (SEALS or special agents for instance), is isolation, which you can divide into two groups:

1) segmentation
2) punctuality

Segmentation comes down to dividing the timeline into smaller segments - the more a given situation is uncertain and chaotic, the more of smaller segments you will need. Steven Billy Mitchell, aka Andy McNab - English writer and ex-special forces soldier - says that he made it through the brutal selection to SAS because "today" was the only thing that mattered to him. It wasn't important at all if he was a zero or a hero yesterday - yesterday was non-existent history.

It is just "today" that matters. Today is the only day that you have - after a fashion - control over. There's no tomorrow, so don't let your mind drive you there.

The trick is to treat every day like a single railcar. If you must exercise six times a week - then according to this logic - you just exercise once, repeating it six times.

The route I usually run is 1 mile. I usually do 5 miles - in this case I don't go out to run five rounds - I go out to run one round five times. The difference may look subtle to you - but it works. You just divide the whole train into railcars.

McNab says that he still divides his day into 3 hour segments. He only pays attention to what he has to do over these next 3 hours. He handles the next 3 hours just after the first segment passes. Thus, during the day he has eight mini-days.

Punctuality means that - isolating again - you just focus on a given single stretch of reality. You concentrate on what's neutral or positive. If it is problematic for you - you pay attention to what's new in the given moment.

An extreme example - when guards put a cocked gun into McNab's mouth, he had two choices - allow his mind to obsess over what was going to happen to him if the gun fired (or they shot him intentionally), or focus on punctually. He chose the second option, concentrating just on the taste of the steel in his mouth. He passed the entire awareness onto the small chosen stretch of reality perceived with his senses. Almost always - if you're still alive - in this very moment, in this very second, everything's alright.

Isolation - either through segmentation or punctuality - is as a matter of fact a pure mindfulness - not used as a practice or an art, but more for practical and down to earth purposes. The faith in what your own special effects department (your mind) brings you can be very stressful. And if you have to cheat yourself, lie in a less stressful and detrimental way.

Celebrate!

You need to celebrate your own life - every single day.

Here's a quick idea that will help you feel good. **The conscious creation of moments of joy and pleasure.** First for you, then for the others. Celebrate all these small things - it could be making your green tea or coffee exactly as you like it, creating a whole ritual around its preparation and consumption. Or putting your best clothes on, spraying yourself with your best fragrance and going to a theater or your favorite restaurant. Make this moment special and make it "your thing." Have this "thing" regularly.

Start with small things, then focus on the bigger stuff.

This way you create a habit of creating your own moments of joy.

A Few Simple Techniques (and some more philosophy)

-Throughout your day, consciously and deliberately remove the tension from your body. Do it regularly. One of the easiest ways is to introduce the alpha waves and one of the most effective and quickest techniques is this:

-Sit down

-Tighten all the muscles you possibly can and hold like this for ten seconds. Then release.

-Take three deep and slow breaths (inhale - pause - exhale - repeat three times)

-Close your eyes.

-Relax for a few minutes.

Repeat this during your day at the times when you feel tension or stress.

-The next technique/idea is called "The Chocolate Voice." It's funny, and great if you love to torture yourself with internal dialogues.

What's your favorite food? Chocolate? Ice cream? Something that makes you feel good when you just think about it. Something that you start eating and say, "Uummmmm… Yeeeaah…"

Let's say that it is chocolate.

Imagine how you feel. What do you experience when you start eating it? Where do these feelings begin, how do they spread around your body? What do you feel and how do you feel? What kind of voice do you use in your self-talk?

Let me guess - gentle, slow, warm, almost a bedtime type of voice. You don't just throw out the word "chocolate." It's more likely "chooo-coooo-laaa-teeee…" You can imagine that you are recording a radio commercial and that you need to dub a voice. Let it be sensual and deep.

Do you have it? Do it now.

Once you set what you feel (chocolate feelings) and how your chocolate voice sounds - you can try telling yourself anything else, but your attempts to bring yourself down and be negative with this voice in your head will be totally absurd and ridiculous. Remember your chocolate voice and use it frequently.

-Affirmations. A very powerful thing.

Whenever you feel that your mind is racing and you're resisting the present moment, feeling uncomfortable and looking for the solution in the next moment, you can use these simple mantras/affirmations:

-> *It is perfectly fine to be here. Everything I do leads me to something bigger.*

-> *I fully accept myself and I fully accept this moment. I fully accept my emotions and thoughts, allowing myself to peacefully experience everything that's inside and around me.*

-> *I am grateful to be here now and I'm grateful for who I am.*

->*This very moment is everything I have. I fully accept it and allow it to be. There is no sense in resisting what already IS.*

And so on - you can also come up with your own affirmations and you can use them throughout the day, during various tasks, to set your mind to this type of Zen thinking. They also prove helpful during meditation. You can use them as an anchor to the present moment, instead of counting to ten or focusing on any given object.

-Another interesting idea is called "the gyroscope rule." A gyroscope is a strange-looking thing that roams and swings from one side to another. In short - if the top goes right, then the bottom goes left.

If you feel that a wave of negative emotions is taking control over you - **feel its direction and invert it.** If your emotions overflow your body from the arms and down, release them in the opposite direction. Emotions always have direction - they are energy. They go in circles. Reflect on the direction and then invert it. It may sound strange at the beginning, but if you focus on how your emotions are, you will understand.

Anger is another interesting and strong emotion. Treat it like a call to inquiry and verification of your goals. It is not that the world doesn't do what you expect it to do. It's just that your expectations are not in accord with how reality works. Interesting, isn't it? Don't get mad here, just reflect on this and take your time to fully understand.

Don't look at the problems. Look for what has to happen for the outcome to be how you expect it to be. Look for what's missing to make your plan come true.

Think about it - how does your internal mechanism work that it causes anger to look like the best solution? Negative emotions are often the effect of our lazy assumption that the result you get comes from the above and is established forever.

Take the following attitude: "No matter what happens, I can handle it."

No matter what happens, treat it like a resource to build a better and bigger future starting NOW.

You have to believe that everything will be alright. You have to TRAIN
yourself to do this. You always have to be bigger than the

circumstances. **And always plan that no matter what, you will still stay in the game.**

Buddhism teaches us that we have to accept that "the suffering is" - life is a struggle and "everybody hurts." As I stated before, we have to experience both the bad and good things to live fully. The truth here is that the "positive thinking" thing is not really Zen. If you like "The Secret" and read about the "Law of Attraction," it's good as long as it serves you, cheers you up and helps you stay positive, and visualization is really extremely powerful, but the point being that you won't build your happiness on just wishful thinking. The real power lies in the **objective thinking and deep understanding (and often NOT thinking, when not necessary),** along with the power of **POSITIVE DOING (TAKING ACTION)** detached from your emotions. **So it's all about POSITIVE DOING.**

Apply it.
Recover your choice.

Avoiding Drama

Despite what some people may think, drama does not look for them. Some of us seem to be living a life filled with non-stop drama. It may be because we are actively seeking it, or actively making it. When we turn our attention inward, to where it should be, we can then live drama-free. We need to let go of everything that is not involved in living the current moment of life; anything dramatic is a distraction. Most drama is derived from the past or future, this person or that person, keeping us from focusing on ourselves and the reality of the moment. This keeps us from taking action and changing our lives.

When we practice Zen, we find peace and joy within ourselves, as opposed to finding these things somewhere else. We learn about ourselves, we clear out the cloudiness of the world, in order to gain a clear understanding of what makes us happy. Keeping our focus on what is happening right now will alleviate most, if not all, of the drama in our lives. Drama consists of what was, and what might be, *not* what REALLY *is*. As I wrote earlier, it's mostly making a problem out of the problem that we made a problem and labeling things as "bad" and "fatal", when they just are what they are. And then looking for all the proofs possible that our judgments about this situation were correct and it's really that bad (because how could we be wrong? Our egos always want to be right, even if it makes no sense and destroys our lives).

Most disagreements and conflicts arise when we lose sight of the importance of self. When we allow others' actions to dictate or affect our reactions, we let drama get the best of us. In Zen the responsibility is placed on self. This may seem like it would be a narrow minded perspective, but when you take the actions of others out of the equation, living drama-free is much easier. Like my mother used to say when I would get all riled up over how other people behaved, "The only person you have real control over is yourself." By removing the focus of what others are doing, we are able to put 100%

of our energy into addressing and experiencing real life, as opposed to fake drama.

When we have peace within ourselves, we have no reason to create drama for the purpose of manipulating others. When we are happy and practicing a Zen lifestyle, there is no reason to try and get others to feel sorry for us. We are able to be content and happy within ourselves, negating the need for sympathy or attention. Practicing Zen allows us to be cheerful with ourselves, we no longer require drama to manipulate people around us into giving us comfort or confirmation.

Honesty is a key aspect of Zen. Honesty also is a huge part of negating drama in your life. When you are honest and open with others, they will feel comfortable trusting you, and much conflict arises out of lack of trust. This includes speaking badly about others or spreading rumors. If you want to live-drama free, the key is to be as real, transparent, and honest as possible. The lack of emotional clarity and honesty (the so called "inhibition") is a basis of most of the life problems. Hiding or acting will take its revenge on your life. Don't.

Also, when you're experiencing trouble, always ask yourself these three questions:

-What is the worst thing that can possibly happen - the blackest scenario (and what is your exact plan for this scenario)?

-What is the best thing that can possibly happen - the greatest scenario, wishful thinking (and what is your exact plan for this scenario)?

-What will probably happen in the most probable situation - the common sense scenario (as well as, what is your exact plan for this scenario)?

> One of our biggest fears is the lack of control, the fear of the unknown. You can also write down these three questions and your answers, along with bullet points for each (your doubts, your plan, your questions to yourself, etc.). You will feel better.

Pleasure is NOT Happiness

People often make a tragically sad error and mistake pleasure with happiness. Cemeteries are full of people who thought so, with celebrities at the top.

This is how it really is:

-Happiness leads to even more happiness.

-Pleasure leads to pain and suffering.

For example:

You are sad and you want to feel better. Okay - parties, booze, drugs, no diet, no exercising. At the beginning it is very nice and pleasurable.

And then? Everything that used to give you pleasure is now needed in even bigger amounts to just make you feel like a medium-sized crap. To put it differently - the pursuit for pleasure always ends in suffering. Happiness hasn't ever been observed.

So here's the alternative and the Zen way - do you want to feel better? Diet, training, self-development, discipline. At the beginning these are not really fun or pleasurable. After some time? You become a happy and fulfilled person. It's as simple as that.

In short:

- You won't feel happy by adding a number of new pleasures.

- The sole pursuit for pleasure leads to a dark dirty hole filled with a vacuum of frustration and despair.

- Happiness comes from regular WORK and SELF ACTUALIZATION - I'm not necessarily talking about your job, but rather about you working on yourself - your goals, your dreams, personal plans, health, body, relations with other human beings, balanced lifestyle.

Please, for your own good, remember and never forget this.

Accept Everything, Lose Nothing

Life is fluid. It is constantly changing. If we continually resist change, we will create problems and issues that do not need to be there. We need to accept the undisputable fact that things change. Upon doing so, you may find that you are not disappointed on a regular basis. You may also experience having quite a bit more emotional energy, as you will not be putting it into things that are fruitless. Life is constantly flowing, resistance will only drain you and lead to dissatisfaction and unhappiness.

This morning, my alarm did not go off, I sat in traffic for two hours due to an accident on the freeway, and my coffee spilled all over my lap. I was mad, stressed out, and frustrated. Life was not going as it should in my opinion.

In this case, and many other situations in life, if I had just let go and accepted what was, I would not have ruined my own day. I would have put the energy used in being irritated and aggravated into something that would have made me happy. There is no use in fighting life. It just happens sometimes. What we *can* do is consciously accept what is changing and move with it!

No matter how much time and preparation we put into scheduling and structuring our day to day routines, change is bound to happen. Any number of variables will disrupt what we put so much energy into creating. Regardless of how badly we want things to go according to plan, there will always be outside variables that we cannot control.

When we have a monkey wrench thrown into our carefully structured life it can cause us to become stressed, mad, frustrated and disappointed. Sometimes we let one small thing ruin the entire day.

We may not be able to control the way of the world around us, but we can take a different view on things. We have to learn to flow with the ever-changing world around us. The phrase "go with the flow" makes perfect sense to a Zen-Buddhist.
Accept life for what it is instead of what you want it to be. Learn to just let go.

Six Ways to Practically Let Go

1. Be cognizant of your emotions. We have to be aware of what we are thinking without actually thinking the thoughts. When you start to feel angry or frustrated, and you are observing the emotion, it is easy to self-correct and change the way that you are thinking. Journal your emotions. Write down the situation, what happened, how you felt. What did you do? How did it work out? Journaling is a helpful tool in learning about yourself. Don't overdo it, though. I have been keeping my diary for a few years now and it has really changed the way I now perceive the reality, how I'm able to deal with my emotions and thoughts. I started it off as an emotional dump, but then I noticed that something was wrong. Although writing my all bad thoughts and sadness was a good catalyst at the beginning, it really started to make me sad and anxious after a few months, whenever I decided to go through

all of these memories. "Is there really so much pain and sadness in my life? What's wrong with me," I would ask myself numerous times. After another few months, I have finally figured it out - I was focusing on all the negativity in my life, therefore ignoring the majority of all the great and blissful things that were happening in my life. On one hand it appeared really helpful, as I was able to let all my anger and bitterness out, but by doing that, all my focus went to these negative feelings, giving them the most important place in my mind, memory and awareness. After one year of journaling, I decided to change the course - from then on I started to totally ignore all the bad things that had happened to me. The only events from my life that I decided deserved "eternal life" were the good ones. I decided to start my "positivity challenge." If something bad happened, I would just allow myself to experience it fully, think about it for some time (if there was any sense to think about it in the first place - in terms of practical thinking - was I able to learn anything from these bad things and correct my direction to get where I wanted or not? If not, I would just let it go without any further insights), and then ignore it. My journal has changed. If you open a file where all the sweet, good and great moments from your life are all written down in one place, you instantly feel extreme gratitude for your life and just pure happiness. As you are grateful, you start acting differently. You then start reacting differently, both to the good and bad things in your life. You start noticing all the good consequences of all the events that have occurred in your life. Then it gets easier to see the positives. It starts to uplift you and cheer you up on a daily basis. You gain more momentum and go through your life smiling. You then attract more positive people and events. And so the circle of positivity goes. I highly recommend that you commit 10-15 minutes a day to write down all the good things that happened to you. All of these memories that are worth saving. All of these things you are grateful for. Ignore all the bad things. It will bring so much more positivity into your life.

2. Honestly realize and accept the fact that everything is not within your control. Well, duh, we all know this. The problem is we do not accept this concept very easily. Our reactions to our plans being changed by things we cannot control usually come in the form of anger and frustration. The first step to really grasping the fact that we cannot control everything is to understand that things WILL happen that are out of our control. Obsessing over something you can't change is just a huge waste of your time and energy.

It's really all about how you interpret things. Perception is your reality. The way you perceive the world and process all the information in your mind is going to decide how happy will you be.

The problem with our culture and society is that we always want to pigeonhole all the events in our life - we think that they are either good or bad, which is rarely true. Buddhism teaches us that the majority of our problems come from our wrong perception of reality. The "good" and "bad" doesn't really exist. The duality is not real. It's just our intrusive need to label everything around us and to judge. The majority of things in our existence just are what they are. Since you can't change what already is, you can't change the present moment, there's no other way but to just accept both the "good" and "bad."

And if you want to be happy, you will have to start noticing the "good" in the "bad." It's really up to you how you interpret things. It's just another ability to learn, just like swimming or riding a bike. How we label things is going to determine how we feel. Notice that whenever you come across things you describe as "bad," all this resistance ("I don't want this, why did this happen to me," etc.), creates even more negativity and makes you feel even more miserable. It is mostly your interpretation of each event and thing that really makes the "bad" feel so bad. It is our egos that want the control - "how come this happened to ME? I don't want anything bad happen to ME. I want to control EVERYTHING in my life!" Of course, we've been socially conditioned to see certain things in our lives as bad. For example, the death of a family member is perceived as bad by 99.99% of the people I know. But death has been around forever and we can't change it. Granted, it makes us feel really bad, but that's one of the things that we just have to accept. As a matter of fact, all this sadness and grief is also a part of our culture and social conditioning - in some countries and cultures the funerals include happy music and cheerful dancing all night long as the people believe that the dead person is now in a better place and will live in happiness forever, so it's a perfect reason to celebrate, especially because the person wouldn't want to see family members and friends depressed and crying. You see - the same inevitable thing, just different perceptions. When we lose someone, even if it's "just" a divorce or split-up, it's mainly our broken attachment to the person that hurts. Our ego. The rest just is what it is. You have the power and you have the right to interpret your reality however you choose to. This is one of the biggest secrets of happiness. You are the one who perceives and interprets the reality - the reality that without you just is what it is. If you choose to look for just the good things in the seemingly bad situations, you WILL find them. Look for the good things! Train your perception to detect them. It won't be easy and will need lots of energy initially, but it's your perception that determines your emotions and how you feel in general.

3. See the big picture. When things go awry, try to look at the event from a broader perspective. You come home expecting to get ready for a big date, and the pipes in the bathroom blow. Your car blows a hose on the way to work. Your boss schedules you to work on a day you counted on taking the kids to the zoo. When we look at these events in the moment, they seem astronomically disturbing and earth-shattering. Yet, if we take a step back, and view them from a wider view, they do not seem so significant. View your problems from an alien's perspective staring down at the earth... they are not nearly as devastating. In six months, a year, ten years from now, whatever happened will not be that big of a deal.

Again, keeping a journal will help you see all these connections and results of each action and event. You will be able to read your life as a book. It will be easier for you to see how funny some of your "big problems" look after a few months or years. And even if they were not funny at all, you might notice that almost everything happens in our life for a reason - to guide us, teach us and make us stronger.

A few years ago I was heavily depressed. My mind was full of all these questions and thoughts like "why does my life suck so much, I don't know what else I can do, I can't take it anymore." It was one of the darkest times of my life and I was dangerously close to serious suicidal thoughts. But the most brutal suffering is often what brings the most positive and transformative change. When you're in the middle of it, you can't see it from the bigger perspective, as in these situations you're emotionally inefficient and it's often too "dark" to see the meaning. Little did I know that all the terrifying suffering was one of the best things that has ever happened to me - I would have never gotten where I am right now if not for that depression I had to overcome. I would probably never realize one of the most important things in my life, I wouldn't start really working to make my life better and I would now literally be someone else - weaker, softer, less focused, less determined and more scared of everything. It has made me evolve.

Now, as I'm able to see things more clearly I see that there's no good or bad - we have the power to label anything as we please so that it helps us to be happy. Practically all of the "bad" things that happened to me have eventually led to something great and worth the suffering. All the dead-end jobs, bad choices and seemingly dead-end life roads have eventually lead me somewhere and showed me something really valuable. Start looking for the good in your life, because it's always there, no matter what. Start asking yourself "what can I learn from this situation? What is good about this? Where can it possibly lead me someday?" And whenever you find yourself trapped in the negative thoughts and emotions, force yourself to stop and ask "what am I focusing on right now? How does it help me? Why should I perceive this situation in a negative light when it's just making me feel bad?" That's a habit that you have to develop. Once you do this, you will be a much happier person. You will be able to notice beauty in everything around you, in yourself too.

4. Accept that we cannot control people as well as situations. This is especially true for the relationships we have with people close to us or the people that we come in contact with every day. Our loved ones (kids, husband, wife, family, boy/girlfriends) are involved in our everyday comings and goings, and eventually are bound to act in a way that we do not like or understand. The people we work with, be it a supervisor or coworker, are inevitably going to do something that we do not care for. We have to accept the people around us: what they say, what they do, and who they are. You should fully accept all these behaviors (if you have to hang around these people, of course) without any judgments and with forbearance. If you don't really like these people, remember: you are doing it for yourself as well. You can't really change a person

until they want to change themselves. You can't do the work for someone. Zen teaches us that everyone is responsible for their own actions, so that you need to change your mind maps from "it's the other people that make me feel this way" to "I make me feel this way." It will give you a superpower - the ability to understand and take responsibility for your own emotions and actions.

5. Find the humor in the situation. This is one of the ways I have learned to accept and let go. I see the situation that I am in from the outside and laugh just as if it was a funny movie or TV show. Finding the funny side of a problem allows us to detach and step back from situations that go wrong. When you are amidst situations that have gone badly, it is easy to be mad and aggravated. Yet, once you pull yourself away and take the time to look at it from another perspective, you can usually find most things to be comical.

Do you know what helps me? Whenever I feel sad and bad about something, whenever I become a whining, self-piteous little pathetic creature, I start laughing at myself, big time. Self-distance is the best medicine for all these slimy negative emotions. Once I went to another country just to take a part in a seminar. I was to give a 20 minute speech about self-development in Prague, Czech Republic. Before the event started, I went out to see the city and do some sightseeing. When I was eating dinner, I accidentally spilled a whole bowl of yellow pea soup on my white shirt and gray trousers. I looked like I didn't make it to the toilet or drank way too much vodka for my stomach to handle it. I momentarily become super angry and frustrated, as the time was short and there was no possibility to go to my hotel room and change, or to buy new clothes, so I had to perform like that in front of more than 100 people. But then when I was just about to resign, go back to my hotel and spend the night watching movies, whipping myself emotionally, I thought, "I didn't take this opportunity and this flight just to let a bowl of stupid cream pea soup ruin it. I'm here in this beautiful city and tonight I'm going to help people change the way they see the world." But guess what? I was still angry. My hands were shaking, I was all sweaty and I looked like an idiot. I couldn't perform in this negative emotional state. So I started imagining that the voice in my head sounded like Cartman from *South Park*. "Ohhh noooo! Muum! Muuuum?!... My little sweet trip is ruined! Don't you see guys!? This is WRRROONG! So WROOOOOOONG!" Then I imagined that if someone laughs at me during my speech, I will shout "RESPECT-MY-AUTHORITY!" That made me burst into laughter and the waiter who just happened to pass me by probably thought that there was something wrong with me. Then I changed the pitch and made the worried voice in my head sound like Mickey Mouse. Now all my little petty complaints about how I ruined *my sweet little trip* sounded even funnier. "Oh no! Mum, look! I have peed all over my little sweet boy pants! What am I going to do now? The kids in the sandbox are going to laugh at me!" And so on. Ultimately, all my worries got so ridiculed and surreal that I couldn't continue them without laughing out loud. And you know what? The seminar and my speech went just great. Even though I looked like a disaster and there were a few laughs from the audience before I started, I was totally positive, and after I finished, the applause totally exceeded my expectations. I threw a joke about my stupid look, and people started laughing. After the event came to an end, I approached a beautiful girl and said, "Hey, look . . . I peed all over my sweet little boy pants." I was just like, "who cares, I don't know anyone in this city and we all die anyway." Not that I was expecting a great reaction, but believe it or not, she started giggling and we had a great conversation. After that, we went out for a beer and I met her friends, totally cool people. Now I have great friends to visit in Prague. That was one of the best evenings I had that year, all this in my trousers and shirt with yellow pea cream spilled all over them. It is really all about your emotions and how you handle them. Given the same situation, I might as well have started saying, "Oh no, it is always like that, the world hates me, why did this happen to me? I was hungry, I wanted to eat this soup, now it's all on my trousers, how am I going to clean that? How am I going to give my speech? Why am I so unlucky, oh no, not now, blah-blah-blah." That would obviously just make things much worse, leading to a downward spiral of self-punishment and negativity. I wouldn't have given my speech, I wouldn't have met all these great people and I would have felt sorry for weeks, if not months afterwards. Don't fall into negativity, which leads nowhere. Cheer up and make fun of yourself. Don't play "Mr. Serious Bond, James Bond" all the time.

6. Finally, reflect on these universal laws of nature and accept them. How do they apply to your life?

Acceptance - Things are what they are. Just like that. Everything is neutral. The nature doesn't know the intention. A random event doesn't know the intention. Things happen. Nothing is either good or bad. To live fully, you have to accept fully. The suffering IS. Life is not perfect. But without the acceptance, it won't be lived fully.

Action - Life is movement. In nature, things happen without planning. Actions are always sincere and simple. No need for intent or calculation. It's just enough to see the direction. An external activity.

Emptiness - The peace inside. Silence and stillness. No expectations. Lack of commitment and involvement. As life can't stand a vacuum, emptiness is immediately filled. Emptiness cannot be self-serving or calculated. It either is empty or it is not.

Acceptance. Action. Emptiness. That's how nature works.

Why is Being Alone a Good Thing?

There is a big difference between loneliness and solitude. Loneliness is painful. Loneliness can actually be experienced when you are still around people. It is a how we feel when we do not have connections and contact with others. We feel as if we do not belong and are not accepted. Solitude, on the other hand, is a very beneficial and constructive thing to indulge in. When we engage in solitude, we can find enjoyment in being alone. It is a time to focus inward and engage yourself.

A main difference between the two is in how we view ourselves. We can be our own best company. Solitude helps us to develop a healthy sense of who we are. We become the center of our own attention, the captain of our own ship. We need to take the time to see that we are still in charge of our lives. It's essential that we use moments of solitude to keep from becoming overwhelmed and drained by external stimuli.

Solitude provides us with:

- Time to deal with our emotional issues
- Time to think without interruption
- Time to learn more about ourselves
- Time to indulge our creativity
- Time away from others allows us to find out who we are

How to go into solitude:

1. Choose a time. It doesn't matter when, just choose a time when you can actually be alone, undisturbed. How long? As

long as possible, using your common sense. Remember though, it is about the quality of time, not the quantity.

2. Choose a place. Of course, it is best to get out of your everyday environment, but if you can't there are ways to find solitude in your current surroundings. If you choose to stay at home or in your office, make sure that you will not be interrupted. You could also choose to go out to the beach, a park, the mountains, a lake... you get the idea.

Other ideas:

- Read a book.
- Give yourself some spa time and take a long, hot bath.
- Go for a run or a walk, without music.
- Get up an hour before the rest of your household or go into work an hour or two before everyone else.
- Try going into solitude at the same time every day.

What to do while you are in solitude?

- Meditate

Being alone in a quiet environment is the perfect backdrop for meditation. And of course in Zen, meditation is key to getting to know and find our true selves.

- Think Creatively

When we have a clear mind and quiet surroundings, our creative minds can run freely. There is no one to judge you, no one to distract you. Some of the most innovative, ground breaking ideas were conceived during moments of solitude.

- Connect with Nature

When you are alone and undistracted, it is much easier to appreciate the wonders of nature. Let yourself fully experience all that is around you. Feel the grass and dirt under your feet, listen to the rustling leaves, smell the water, watch the birds. When we are grounded and fully connected to the world around us, we can intimately bond with ourselves.

These moments of solitude can really change your personality and how you perceive the world. **You should be alone regularly, but I also recommend that for once in your life you try an extended period of solitude.**

After I graduated from the university, I decided not to continue on to obtain an MA, but to pack my backpack and hit the road instead. I decided to go to Morocco, as it has always been my dream to see the Sahara desert and spend a night there. What's important here is that I didn't take my laptop, smartphone nor mp3 player with me. It was just me, my backpack with some clothes, sleeping bag and medicines, a map and a whole lot of time for my thoughts and meditations.

Since then, I have traveled a lot in many different countries, as traveling has become one of my biggest passions ever, but no trip was even close to that one when it comes to deepness or when I look at how it has changed me. I was all alone for the first time in my life, in a stranger country, first time in my life on a different continent. I didn't know French and I didn't know Arab or Berber language. I had no friends or relatives there. I didn't know too much about Arab and Muslim culture. My budget was very low. I had no other choice but to interact with people, to spend all my days wandering through the crowded narrow medieval streets, big cities and empty sandy plains, to spend all my day on buses looking through the windows, admiring all these extraordinary views, being present and thinking about my life.

Once I hitchhiked to a remote empty beach on the Atlantic Ocean shore. I just planned to spend one day and one night there, but I forgot about the holy days in the Muslim religion during that month. No bus or taxi was going that route for five days. A few of the other cars I had spotted sitting by the road were totally full of Moroccan families. The only taxi driver that stopped literally wanted me to pay $1500.00 for a 25 mile ride. I was trapped there, so I went to the nearest little town by foot, bought a few bags of fresh fruits, bread, fish and water before everything closed for good, and spent five days and five nights at this beach, all alone. I slept in a hut in a big cave, just a few meters from the raging Atlantic Ocean. My only companions were big white seagull-like birds. That was one of the best things that has ever happened to me. I came to a conclusion about what I really wanted in life. I came to understand that I wanted someone to share all these emotions with, that I wanted to be free to travel wherever and whenever I want (that's when I realized that I needed to start an on-line business), that I needed to learn more languages, because English was not enough, so I decided to learn French and Spanish fluently. The list of my insights was really long. I finally understood who I was.

When you're not distracted by the TV, Internet, smartphones, chores, gossip, jobs, friends, partying and all the other things, the truth that is already inside you (which has always been there), the real essence of who you are can come to the surface much faster. Without that very trip, I would now probably be much less developed when it comes to my self-awareness and personal goals. Maybe I'd still work in an office, doing the 9-5 that I hated. Thanks to one-and-a-half months of solitude, silence and meditation, the waters of my mind became still and I was finally able to see the bottom, to see the blue sky, when all these dark clouds disappeared for a few moments. Does it mean that you have to go to Morocco, India or some other distant country in order to do that? Of course not.

If you can - do it! If not - you can just find other ways. Once every few months I pack my tent and some canned food and set off to a nearby forest. I usually spend 2-3 days there, walking all day long in the wild, sleeping in a tent, meditating a lot, being thankful for the beauty that's surrounding me. That really helps. If you don't like forests or extended travel, think of anything else that would please you. The possibilities are limitless.

At the center of your being you have the answer; you know who you are and you know what you want. - Lao Tzu

De-clutter and Live Simply

Emotional Clutter

Don't be a hoarder. We all accumulate things in life, events, emotions, traumatic experiences. Most people hang on to all of those things. They accumulate them to almost astronomical proportions.

This can be easily compared to someone who fills their home with items until their home is almost unlivable. Such items include but are not limited to trash, food items, meaningless trinkets, and so on. For some reason, these people have an attachment to these things and cannot let them go, no matter how much more difficult their living situations become. These piles and piles of belongings get in the way of functioning in everyday life and make the easiest task a difficult one. Sure, walking across a normal living room is easy, but, if you fill it 6 feet high with "stuff," walking from point A to point B can prove to be a pain, if not dangerous. Going to the bathroom? Sure, that is easy in a clutter-free home, but many hoarders cannot even access the bathroom, let alone get into it and use it. It is hard to move around in such a crowded space. Many times, these people become trapped.

The hoarder scenario is not unlike the same problems that we face in everyday life when we have not yet learned how to let go and de-clutter our inner self. We hold onto things, pile up trash that we do not need, and hang onto things that will hinder us when we are trying to move around within our inner self.

More often than not, we start to believe that these events and emotions that we have collected make us who we are. We have accumulated all of these things and as we look inside ourselves, they obscure our vision. Our hoarding affects our line of sight; how we view ourselves. It is like gazing into a home where trash and meaningless objects have been accumulated for many years, all you can see are possessions piled sky high. This emotional hoarding distorts the view of who we are. Just because events have taken place in our lives and things have happened to us does not mean that this is the definition of who we are. Or even worse, by holding onto these things, we can become them.

The object of de-cluttering your hoarded, emotional house is to be able to get a clear picture or reflection of yourself. When looking at a hoarder's home, can you see the beautiful architecture, the fabulous hardwood flooring, the crown molding? Probably not. You will see trash, feces, and leftover garage sale fodder. When we hoard experiences, our mind will reflect those, instead of reflecting what we are experiencing right now: life, the epitome of Zen. When things are in their natural state, they reflect what is currently happening, not things that happened previously. A still lake reflects what is directly above it at the time. Wouldn't it be strange to see something reflecting on the surface that was there yesterday, three months ago, or five years ago? When practicing Zen, we want to get back to our true nature. We want to see a reflection of ourselves in our natural state: our real self. The only way to do that is to get rid and let go of past experience. We must de-clutter ourselves on the inside.

Once we get rid of this emotional clutter we can see reality for what it is, instead of gauging everything from behind the veil of past experience. The feelings and events that we accumulate work as a filter, distorting our view of reality. We start to believe that everything that we are feeling is real. When actually the only thing that is real is the very moment we are experiencing, not the past, and certainly not the future.

Practicing Zen meditation will allow you to clean out yourself, de-clutter your spirit, and allow you to see yourself for who you really are. Meditation is not designed to fix ourselves; it is designed to remind us of who we really are. It is not practiced to achieve enlightenment, per say; it allows you to use and express your already enlightened nature that is buried under all the clutter. We must learn to practice meditation by living life as it is right now, every day, every moment. Practice mediation all day long; incorporate it into every moment of your life. Whatever you are engaged in, go at it 100 percent. The more you do, the faster you will get rid of all of the clutter.

The things that have happened to us in our lives are not permanent, or we would say that they are *"happening,"* instead of that they *"happen-ed."* The more that we fixate our view of self on the past, the more we are limiting our thoughts, ideas, and actions. The narrower that our view is of who we are, the more limited our options and solutions to life's circumstances will be.

When meditating deeply, you will able to connect with your updated version of yourself, which will enable you to function in a natural state. In the natural world everything just functions, "naturally." When we are able to clearly, connect with our true nature, we will simply function. We can act spontaneously. We are free of the active thinking that confuses us, leaving us not knowing what to do. We will be able to act intuitively. We will be unchained from unhappiness, regret, and tripping up. Get rid of all of your clutter and live life to the fullest by connecting with and trusting your true nature.

Practical De-Cluttering

- Start with small goals, in short intervals. 10-15 minutes is a good place to start. This is enough time to clean out a drawer, clean off a shelf, or file a pile of papers.
    1. Start by clearing everything off or out of that designated space.
    2. Now, throw away, donate, sell, or repurpose the rest.

De-cluttering an entire room or home may seem like a daunting task, but when you break it up into quarter-hour intervals, it may be easier than you think. This bit of motivation found in the form of accomplishment may very well be what you need to get the ball rolling. Pick a different area to work on each week.

- Do not focus on making things perfect. You need to just focus on making your life simpler.
- De-clutter your life by getting rid of unnecessary commitments. Only keep the most important commitments you have. Learn how to say no to new commitments. Be more selfish with your time.
- Look at how much time you are spending checking email, watching
vlogs, reading blogs, social networking etc. Can you live without some of them? If yes, get rid of them. If the answer is no, limit the time that you devote to these things. Check email only twice a day. Browse Facebook for 15 min.

It is just as important for us to de-clutter our lives as it is to de-clutter our minds. Living Zen is the epitome of living simply. The more minimalistic your life, the more freely you will be able to truly live it. Zen teaches us that we shouldn't cling to material possessions. It's all temporary. It's all energy consuming. **Zen is about knowing what you really need in your life and staying with just that.** It protects you from greed, paying too much attention to material things and from distraction.

Whenever I start a new stage in my life, I always update all my surroundings. All the things you decide to keep even though you don't use and need them just hold you back and slow you down. They diminish your clarity. When I finished the university and wasn't sure what my next move should be, I started with a total de-clutter. I sold all of my furniture, as I came to the conclusion that I hadn't been using 90% of it for the last three years. They were just objects that gathered dust, useless gadgets and way too much memorabilia. I bought myself a new desk, which was basically a minimalistic thin wide piece of black-colored wood standing on a two metal legs with nothing else to it. I already had my Kindle, so I decided to sell the majority of my books - at least those that I didn't plan to read again. Then I reviewed my wardrobe and came to the conclusion that I only wear about 10% of what's inside. I packed up the rest of my clothes and gave them to charity. If you haven't worn something for years, what makes you think that you will suddenly start someday? This process lasted for a few weeks (every single day I would throw out, sell or give away one or more things from my room). I gradually started feeling better as this process progressed. When I finished, I discovered that I can pack ALL that I materially own in my life (except for my music-recording gear and guitar . . . and the furniture, obviously, but it's nothing more than the unnecessary basics which I could easily leave behind at any moment), in one 35 liter backpack and one medium suitcase. My room was now clean, tidy, spacious, perfectly organized and I felt totally refreshed. It was much easier to gather my thoughts, create, work, study and think about what to do next. I wasn't busy with all these things that would just draw away more of my attention and energy. Since then, I do this kind of review at least once a year. Whenever I am planning for something big or committing to a life-changing decision, I do this.

Recently I have done the same to all my digital data. I organized all my photos, movies and music in one place and got rid of hundreds of gigabytes of useless junk.

Your environment is the projection of what's inside of your mind. If your mind is cluttered, uneasy and neglected, then it's quite possible that your home will look chaotic. If you want to help yourself, de-clutter your environment and all the other areas of your life.

Note that this might also work with your social contacts. If you used to hang out with someone, but for some reason it doesn't serve you anymore and you just feel worse anytime you meet with these people, just stop contacting them or cut it down to the necessary minimum. However obvious it might sound, I'm always totally surprised whenever I find out how many people still hang out with "friends" they now almost hate, just because "they're old friends." Respect yourself, respect your time and respect your mind. Cut out wilted passions and old hobbies that no longer serve you and no longer make you happy. Cut out the food that doesn't serve you. Cut out your job if it makes you miserable. No, not right now . . . find another way to earn enough to pay for your food, shelter and bills first, but come up with a PLAN to ultimately do it. The feeling of control will keep you focused, present and clear.

This is what you do if you want to get ahead. Completely cut out everything that doesn't support you!

Chapter 4: Where Do I Start? How To Practice Zen as an Ordinary Person

Practicing something entails that we repetitiously engage in an activity so that we can develop a skill. Practice is an integral part of learning anything new. Eventually, practicing an activity will enable you to preform it without even thinking. Practitioners of Zen both *practice* a skill set, and refer to the result of developing and employing this skill set as their *practice*.

Now that you have more of a grasp of Zen and what living and practicing Zen entails, here are some practical things you can do when starting a Zen practice:

- Start now! Do not procrastinate. It will pay off.
- Meditate. It can't be said enough - learn how, do it often, make it a part of your everyday life. Learn from this book, other books, and online videos, visit a Zen temple, go on a Zen retreat. Take lessons from Zen teachers. Delve into the world of meditation. You must take direction from others who know what they are doing because you can end up causing yourself more problems if you don't. All too often, unskilled or uniformed meditators spend their time going over past experiences, fantasizing, rehashing problems, or emotionally connecting with past trauma. Find an experienced instructor through any avenue you feel most comfortable with.

- Find a Zen temple or retreat that is local. Research the authenticity of the Zen teacher. Find out what school it is, what country it came from, what ideals they hold most important. If you are interested in a monastery, find one. Otherwise, find a place that embraces the Zen layman. Find what is most comfortable for you.
- Practice, practice, practice!

Five Things to Make Sure You Do:

1. Make choices. For each question that pops up in day to day life, there are a numerous amount of options. Don't let numerous amounts of solutions and scenarios dance around in your head for extended periods of time. It will only drain your energy and confuse you. Do not over think. Do not regret. Just do. Choose, obligate yourself to your choice, and stick with it. If at any point your choice does not seem to be working, choose another option. Do not waste your time rehashing, worrying, or coming up with a million other solutions and why they may not work. Make a choice. You can either believe that something is very difficult and almost impossible to accomplish or that it's extremely easy. In both scenarios you are probably wrong, but guess in which case it will be easier for you to succeed?
2. Phase out a dualistic perspective. We should not label anything. There is nothing good, nor nothing bad. Nothing is either right or wrong. The world just *is*. Stop labeling and judging. Act out of intuition, and carry on living your life.

3. Quit multi-tasking for good. You will never be able to be fully engaged in anything. In order to truly live life, and experience what it means to be Zen, you need to give each thing you are doing your full attention. When we multi-task our attention is all over the place. We end up not focusing on any one thing and draining ourselves in the process. This is not living because we are not able to fully engage in any said moment or task. I belong to a few self-development groups where we exchange our experiences on time management, different business ideas, learning techniques, psychology and so on. One of the members once posted a thread on-line where he asked how to organize time so that you can handle more than four or five areas of your life every single day. Well . . . you can't. Unless you are Napoleon Bonaparte, your day is 78 hours long, you inherited billions or you don't have to sleep and eat. Zen is hugely about the right amount of concentration and focus, and you can't really focus on all the things that you want in life at once. When I was working 9-5, going to gym and staying on a diet to gain some weight, I couldn't really do anything more than that. I just didn't have time. Like AT ALL. And I would sleep just 6 hours every night (sometimes less). If someone is focusing on everything at once, he probably is not good at anything at all. When I quit my job I was sure that I would have more time during the day and be able to do all these things (learn languages, go to the gym, watch movies, keep up with my diet, meet friends, record music, relax, sleep 8 hours a day, etc.), but in reality, I was just able to work on developing my business, eat, keep my place clean, do some shopping and meet my girlfriend. You just need to decide which areas of your life are crucial and which need most of your

attention. Then - sacrifice yourself and make them work. If you decide to focus on the financial/career aspects and sports, there won't be too much time left for other things, no matter how well you are organized, unless you want to suck at those things or achieve your goals at an extremely slow pace. You still have to sleep, eat, do some cleaning, shopping, go to the doctor sometimes, drive from point A to B, wait in traffic jams and so on, and sometimes, even if you are a born go-getter, achiever and a titan of hard work, you will still need to relax and pause. If you have your own family, you will have even less free time.

Remember - something that is very important and something I just understood when I was 25 - if you put too much weight on your back, you will just end up overworked, frustrated and will hardly achieve anything, as you need to just focus on two things at once. Yes TWO, maybe three, if the third thing isn't something big. So it could be money, relationships, the gym (or some other sport) plus a well-organized diet, if you know how to prepare your healthy meals in batches, ahead of time. Or it could be learning a new language, working on your music project and studying for your degree. But it will really be difficult to focus on anything else if you want to do well and be successful. It also often happens that your new goal might be interesting and worth achieving, but totally incongruent with your other goals, which will eventually slow you down in all the other areas or make you fail. Choose goals that go well with your overall long-term vision of yourself. Dividing your focus between too many things will cause frequent burn-outs and lack of motivation, which will eventually lead to the conclusion that the direction you have chosen was the wrong one, even when it wasn't. Don't push yourself too hard, don't be this bad cop for yourself. It never leads anywhere. Choose two things in life, focus on them, maintain your discipline, master them to the level that is satisfactory and then focus on the other aspects of your life.

4. Please also remember that you don't really have to do anything. Albert Ellis, the famous American psychotherapist, coined the funny and emphatic term "musturbation." It is an inner conviction that you have to do certain things, they are your obligation and hence you don't have a choice. Your perception becomes your reality. As I wrote before, one of the most stressful situations in the life of a human being occurs when we feel the lack of control - the fear of helplessness. So if you have to do something - "you have no choice" - and additionally you don't really feel like doing that, the inner conflict, stress and pressure appear. You become a victim of the circumstances. And being a victim is not the best position to be in. Why? Because then your faith isn't lying in your hands. The following technique is ingeniously simple and logical. It is classical reframing - the shift of perception from the limitation to the resources.

When psychotherapists studying the art of achievement analyzed the language and thought patterns of the most successful people, they discovered a very interesting thing. Those people never talked about having to do something - they talked about making certain choices, because even if someone puts a gun to your head, you still do have a choice. It can be a crappy choice, but you have it. In this case you can either do what they tell you to do or you can ignore them.

So you always have a choice to take advantage of your own perception - you can either recognize that you are a victim of the circumstances and continue to stress about it - or you can recognize that your life is the result of your own choices. The difference is either slavery or liberty – **it's about putting the responsibility for you on yourself.**

Think about something that you really don't want to do, but you "have to." Reflect on how it feels. Scan and analyze your body. Feel how you perceive this kind of stress. Now, reframe it, remembering that you always have a choice. You don't HAVE TO, you CHOOSE to. It's your choice, and even if you don't feel like doing that - you are the one in charge here. You should feel relieved.

Quit "musturbation" and make your own choices.

Zen is about the right perception.

5. Live Zen. All the time. Being Zen is not like having a hobby or skills that we use some of the time. We don't just employ our knowledge of Zen, or the things that we practice when a problem arises or it is convenient. It truly is the lifestyle of all lifestyles. In order for us

to really live Zen we must commit to applying Zen principles and meditational practices into every moment of our day. We should live a new kind of life: living experiencing life, in the present moment, every second of the day. **We should BE ZEN.**

Conclusion

The two key things to focus on when living a Zen lifestyle are: Zen (meditation), practice and the right mindset. We should learn to live a life where we are constantly living. This must be done with constant meditation. Otherwise, as you very well may know, the modern world and past experiences will keep us from doing so. We must focus our attention on living, and thanks to Zen meditational methods, it is not only possible, but practical in everyday life of a regular person!

I truly hope that you enjoyed this book and found the experience I shared with you helpful. I wish that it is able to transform your thinking and make your life easier and happier.

One last thing before you go – Can I ask you a favor? I need your help! **If you like this book, could you please share your experience on Amazon and write an honest review? It will be just one minute for you (I will be happy even with one sentence!), but a GREAT help for me. Here's the direct link: http://tinyurl.com/reviewmyzenbook.** Since I'm not a well-established author and I don't have powerful people and big publishing companies supporting me, I read every single review and jump around with joy like a little kid every time my readers comment on my books and give me their honest feedback! If I was able to inspire you in any way, please let me know! It will also help me get my books in front of more people looking for new ideas and useful knowledge. If you did not enjoy the book or had a problem with it, please don't hesitate to contact me at contact@mindfulnessforsuccess.com and tell me how I can improve it to provide more value and more knowledge to my readers. I'm constantly working on my books to make them better and more helpful.

Thank you and good luck! I believe in you and wish you all the best on your new journey!

Your friend,
Ian

My Free Gift to You
Discover How to Get Rid of Stress & Anxiety and Reach Inner Peace in 20 Days or Less!

To help speed up your personal transformation, I have prepared a special gift for you!

Download my full, 120 page e-book "Mindfulness Based Stress and Anxiety Management Tools" (Value: $9.99) for free.

Moreover, by becoming my subscriber, you will be the first one to **get my new books for only $0.99,** during their short two day promotional launch. **I passionately write about**: social dynamics, career, Neuro-Linguistic Programming, goal achieving, positive psychology and philosophy, life hacking, meditation and becoming the most awesome version of yourself. Additionally, once a week I will send you insightful tips and **free e-book offers** to keep you on track on your journey to becoming the best you!

That's my way of saying **"thank you"** to my new and established readers and helping you grow. I hate spam and e-mails that come too frequently – **you will never receive more than one email a week! Guaranteed.**

Just follow this link:

http://www.mindfulnessforsuccess.com/positive-psychology-coaching/giveaway.html

Hey there like-minded friends, let's get connected!

Don't hesitate to visit:

-My blog: www.mindfulnessforsuccess.com

-My facebook fanpage:

https://www.facebook.com/mindfulnessforsuccess

-My twitter: https://twitter.com/mindfulness78

Twitter handle: @Mindfulness4Success

-My Instagram profile: https://instagram.com/mindfulnessforsuccess

I hope to see you there!

Recommended Reading For You

If you are interested in Self-Development, NLP, Psychology, Social Dynamics, PR, Soft Skills and related topics, you might be interested in previewing or downloading my other books:

Buddhism: Beginner's Guide: Bring Peace and Happiness to Your Everyday Life

Buddhism is one of the most practical and simple belief systems on this planet and it has greatly helped me on my way to become a better person in every aspect possible. In this book I will show you what happened and how it was.

No matter if you are totally green when it comes to Buddha's teachings or maybe you have already heard something about them - this book will help you systematize your knowledge and will inspire you to learn more and to take steps to make your life positively better!

I invite you to take this beautiful journey into the graceful and meaningful world of Buddhism with me today!

Direct link: http://tinyurl.com/ianbuddhismkindle

Paperback version:

http://tinyurl.com/ianbuddhismpaperback

Meditation for Beginners: How to Meditate (As an Ordinary Person!) to Relieve Stress, Stay Focused, Concentrated and Happy Every Day

Meditation is not necessarily about crystals, hypnotic folk music and incense sticks!

Forget about sitting in unnatural and uncomfortable positions while going "ommmmm...."

It doesn't have to be a club full of yoga masters, Shaolin monks, hippies and new-agers.

It is super practical and universal practice which can improve your overall brain performance and happiness.

When meditating, you take a step back from actively thinking your thoughts, and instead, see them for what they are. The reason why meditation is helpful in reducing stress and attaining peace is that it gives your over-active conscious a break.

Just like your body needs it, your mind does too!

I give you the gift of peace that I was able to attain through present moment awareness.

Direct link: http://tinyurl.com/ianmeditationkindle

Paperback version:
http://tinyurl.com/ianmeditationpaperback

Communication Skills Training: A Practical Guide to Improving Your Social Intelligence, Presentation, Persuasion and Public Speaking

Do You Know How To Communicate With People Effectively, Avoid Conflicts and Get What You Want From Life?

...It's not only about what you say, but also about WHEN, WHY and HOW you say it.

Do The Things You Usually Say Help You, Or Maybe Hold You Back?

Have you ever considered **how many times you intuitively felt that maybe you lost something important or crucial, simply because you unwittingly said or did something, which put somebody off?** Maybe it was a misfortunate word, bad formulation, inappropriate joke, forgotten name, huge misinterpretation, awkward conversation or a strange tone of your voice?

Maybe you assumed that you knew exactly what a particular concept meant for another person and you stopped asking questions?

Maybe you could not listen carefully or could not stay silent for a moment? **How many times have you wanted to achieve something, negotiate better terms, or ask for a promotion and failed miserably?**

It's time to put that to an end with the help of this book.

<u>**Lack of communication skills is exactly what ruins most peoples' lives.**</u>

If you don't know how to communicate properly, you are going to have problems both in your intimate and family relationships.

You are going to be ineffective in work and business situations. It's going to be troublesome managing employees or getting what you want from your boss or your clients on a daily basis. Overall, **effective communication is like an engine oil which** makes your life run smoothly, getting you wherever you want to be. There are very few areas in life in which you can succeed in the long run without this crucial skill.

What Will You Learn With This Book?

-What Are The **Most Common Communication Obstacles** Between People And How To Avoid Them

-How To Express Anger And Avoid Conflicts

-What Are **The Most 8 Important Questions You Should Ask Yourself** If You Want To Be An Effective Communicator?

-**5 Most Basic and Crucial** Conversational Fixes

-How To Deal With Difficult and Toxic People

-Phrases to **Purge from Your Dictionary** (And What to Substitute Them With)

-The Subtle Art of **Giving and Receiving Feedback**

-Rapport, the **Art of Excellent Communication**

-How to Use Metaphors to **Communicate Better** And **Connect With People**

-What Metaprograms and Meta Models Are and How Exactly To Make Use of Them To **Become A Polished Communicator**

-How To Read Faces and **How to Effectively Predict Future Behaviors**

-How to Finally Start **Remembering Names**

-How to Have a Great Public Presentation

-How To Create Your Own **Unique Personality** in Business (and

Everyday Life)

-Effective Networking

Direct Buy Link:

http://tinyurl.com/iancommunicationkindle

Paperback version:

http://tinyurl.com/iancommunicationpaperback

Emotional Intelligence Training: A Practical Guide to Making Friends with Your Emotions and Raising Your EQ

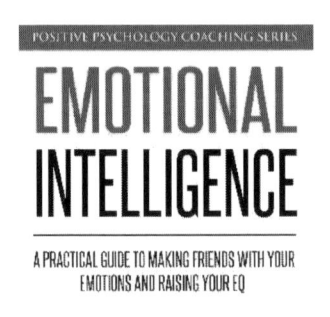

Do you believe your life would be healthier, happier and even better, if you had more practical strategies to regulate your own emotions?

Most people agree with that.

Or, more importantly:

do you believe you'd be healthier and happier if everyone who you live with had the strategies to regulate their emotions?

...right?

The truth is not too many people actually realize what EQ is really all about and what causes its popularity to grow constantly.

Scientific research conducted by many American and European Universities prove that the **'common' intelligence responses account for only less than 20% of our life achievements and successes, while the other more than 80% depends on the emotional intelligence.** To put it roughly: **either you are emotionally intelligent, or you're doomed to mediocrity, at best.**

As opposed to the popular image, emotionally intelligent people are not the ones who react impulsively and spontaneously, or who act lively and fiery in all types of social environments.

Emotionally intelligent people are open to new experiences, can show feelings adequate to the situation, either good or bad, and find it easy to socialize with other people and establish new contacts. They handle stress well, say 'no' easily, realistically assess the achievements of themselves or others, and are not afraid of constructive criticism and taking calculated risks. **They are the people of success.** Unfortunately, this perfect model of an emotionally intelligent person is extremely rare in our modern times.

Sadly nowadays, **the amount of emotional problems in the world is increasing at an alarming rate.** We are getting richer, but less and less happy. Depression, suicide, relationship breakdowns, loneliness of choice, fear of closeness, addictions - this is the clear evidence we are getting increasingly worse when it comes to dealing with our emotions.

Emotional Intelligence is a SKILL, and can be learned through constant practice and training, just like riding a bike or swimming!
This book is stuffed with lots of effective exercises, helpful info and practical ideas.

Every chapter covers different areas of emotional intelligence and shows you, **step by step**, what exactly you can do to **develop your EQ** and become the **better version of yourself**.

I will show you how freeing yourself from the domination of the left-sided brain thinking can contribute to your inner transformation **– the emotional revolution that will help you redefine who you are and what you really want from life!**

In This Book I'll Show You:

-What Is Emotional Intelligence and What Does EQ Consist Of?
-How to **Observe and Express** your Emotions
-How to **Release Negative Emotions** and **Empower the Positive Ones**
-How To Deal With Your **Internal Dialogues**

- How To **Deal With The Past**
- **How to Forgive** Yourself and How to Forgive Others
- How to Free Yourself from **Other People's Opinions and Judgments**
- What Are "Submodalities" and How Exactly You Can Use Them to **Empower Yourself** and **Get Rid of Stress**
- The Nine Things You Need to **Stop Doing to Yourself**
- How to Examine Your Thoughts
- **Internal Conflicts** Troubleshooting Technique
- The Lost Art of Asking Yourself the Right Questions and **Discovering Your True Self!**
- How to Create Rich Visualizations
- LOTS of practical exercises from the mighty arsenal of psychology, family therapy, NLP etc.
- **And Many, Many More!**

Direct Buy Link: http://tinyurl.com/ianeqkindle

Paperback version: http://tinyurl.com/ianeqpaperback

Gain Self-Confidence Fast With NLP

In this short-read you'll learn about the **most effective NLP tools in the context of permanent self-esteem boost**, but also my mindset, the right approach that actually works and I'll share few personal stories that will motivate you. I'll tell you how to stick to your personal change plan and how to start a journey towards being a better person!

Direct link: http://tinyurl.com/ianconfidencekindle

Speed Reading: How to Read 3-5 Times Faster and Become an Effective Learner

No matter if your objective is to **do great during your University exams**, become a **bestselling writer**, or start **your own business,** you will have to read A LOT, and I mean it. Reading takes time. **Time is our most valuable asset** - nothing new here.

You can always make money or meet new friends, but **you will never be able to "make time".** The only way to succeed and have a happy life without regrets is to use it wisely and **learn how to manage and save it.**

In this book, I will take you through the dynamics of speed reading in a way you may have never imagined before. I'm here to preach the need for speed reading and make use of some of the principles that can steer your knowledge and productivity in the right direction.

Learn How To Read 5 Times Faster, Remember Much More and Save Massive Time!

In This Book You Will Read About:
-The History Of Speed Reading
-Popular Speed Reading Myths
-Environment and Preparation
-How To Measure Your Reading Speed
-Key Speed Reading Techniques
-Reading Tips for Computer and Tablet
-Common Reading Mistakes to Avoid
-Easy and Effective Memory/Learning Techniques
-Dealing with Tests and Diagrams
-Practical Exercises and Eye Adjustments
-Useful Links and Ideas

-Diet

-How to Track Your Progress

-Proper Motivation and Mindset

Direct Link: http://tinyurl.com/ianreadingkindle

Paperback Version:

http://tinyurl.com/ianreadingpaperback

About The Author

Author's blog: www.mindfulnessforsuccess.com

Amazon Author Page: http://tinyurl.com/iantuhovsky

Hi! I'm Ian...

...and I am interested in life. In the study of having an awesome and passionate life, which I believe is within the reach of practically everyone. I'm not a mentor or a guru. I'm just a guy who always knew there was more than we are told. I managed to turn my life around from way below my expectations to a really satisfying life, and now I want to share this fascinating journey with you so that you can do it, too.

I was born and raised somewhere in Eastern Europe, where Polar Bears eat people on the streets, we munch on snow instead of ice-cream and there's only vodka instead of tap water, but since I make a living out of several different businesses, I move to a new country every couple of months. I also work as an HR consultant for various European companies. I love self-development, traveling, recording music and providing value by helping others. I passionately read and write about social psychology, sociology, NLP, meditation, mindfulness, eastern philosophy, emotional intelligence, time management, communication skills and all of the topics related to conscious self-development and being the most awesome version of yourself.

Breathe. Relax. Feel that you're alive and smile. And never hesitate to contact me!

Printed in Great Britain
by Amazon.co.uk, Ltd.,
Marston Gate.